# How to Draft Bills Clients Rush to Pay

# How to Draft Bills Clients Rush to Pay

by J. Harris Morgan
edited by Julie Tamminen
with a Postscript by Fran Shellenberger

ABA

SECTION OF LAW PRACTICE MANAGEMENT

Cover design by Catherine Zaccarine.

The Section of Law Practice Management, American Bar Association, offers an educational program for lawyers in practice. Books and other materials are published in furtherance of that program. Authors and editors of publications may express their own legal interpretations and opinions, which are not necessarily those of either the American Bar Association or the Section of Law Practice Management unless adopted pursuant to the By-laws of the Association. The opinions expressed do not reflect in any way a position of the Section or the American Bar Association.

© 1995 American Bar Association. All rights reserved.
Printed in the United States of America.

Library of Congress Catalog Card Number 94-78158
ISBN 1-57073-043-1

00 99 98 97 96   5 4 3 2


Discounts are available for books ordered in bulk. Special consideration is given to state bars, CLE programs, and other bar-related organizations. Inquire at Publications Planning and Marketing, American Bar Association, 750 N. Lake Shore Drive, Chicago, Illinois 60611.

# Foreword

Back in the 1970s, a country lawyer from Greenville, Texas, went on a crusade to revolutionize the practice of law. His message was simple but direct: lawyers in the coming decades would have to run their offices in a more businesslike way. They would need to use machines and systems to improve their efficiency. They would have to track their time in order to place a value on their work. They would have to bill their clients so that the clients perceived real value for the services rendered. This country lawyer assembled an entourage of like-minded practitioners who carried this message throughout the country in a series of programs for practitioners. Because many of the ideas expounded in these road shows have become so ingrained in our professional culture, few people appreciate how radical they were back then.

The country lawyer from Greenville, Texas, was J. Harris Morgan. When I first met Morgan, barely a year out of law school, it was at a program in Houston called "Salvation for the Solo Practitioner." I still remember sitting transfixed by what I was hearing. There was a certain camp-meeting mentality to the proceedings, and the speakers were more like missionaries than CLE lecturers. They believed in their message, and they wanted the audience to believe. And I must confess, I came away a convert.

In the twenty years since our first meeting, J. Harris Morgan has never wavered in his dedication to getting his message out to lawyers. Although there have been changes in technology, forms of practice, public and client attitudes about lawyers, and general acceptance of the basic notion that law is a professional business, the fundamental concepts of Morgan's message ring as true today as they did then.

One of several talks in J. Harris Morgan's repertoire was called, "How to Draft Bills That Clients Rush to Pay." The paradoxical title is intriguing in itself, but the content of the speech was even more amazing: the things that lawyers often thought clients wanted from their lawyers were not necessarily what the clients said they wanted. What clients wanted was demonstrated effort, and they will gladly pay for it. As lawyers, we should listen to the clients, and bill them in such a way that our effort is showcased. Such bills, Morgan argues, clients will rush to pay.

This book does not stop with the general proposition. It goes into specifics about how to accomplish the objective of creating bills that clients really will rush to pay. It is designed to help lawyers craft bills that convey a sense of value and progress to clients—thereby making clients more likely to honor their end of the bargain and pay for the services rendered.

The techniques discussed here not only serve the interests of lawyers; they also serve the public as consumers of legal services. At the heart of the matter is the need for lawyers to do a better job of communicating with their clients, and the bill often ends up being the most visible form of communication between clients and their lawyers. This makes the bill a critical component of the lawyer-client relationship.

The bill is also an important marketing tool. Clients at every stage of their case are more likely to recommend their lawyer's services to others if they have been persuaded that they have received high quality and timely service. This perception can be enhanced by applying the approaches to drafting detailed and action-oriented bills demonstrated by J. Harris Morgan.

The bill is an integral part of any quality management process. Once it is established that the bill is the memorialization of every stage of the client matter, it is possible for the client and the firm to use the bill as a basis for assessing the service delivered. The recitation of work completed in the bill will document the lawyer's accomplishments in a way that makes them easy to monitor.

A detailed bill is more likely to be an honest bill, and an honest bill enhances the firm's reputation for integrity. When partners and associates indicate each step of a transaction, and the time and resources expended, they are accountable for their work in a way that they never are when the bill reads only "For services rendered." The client and the firm can be more confident of the value that was delivered for the fee and expenses charged.

The words of J. Harris Morgan contained in this book can help you to be a better lawyer. Reading and applying the techniques outlined by Morgan will help you to enhance your firm's revenues, client satisfaction, and reputation. J. Harris Morgan understands what it takes to do it right, and now, you can as well.

*Professor Gary A. Munneke*
*Chair, LPM Publishing*

# Contents

FOREWORD     **Gary A. Munneke**     v

CHAPTER **1**     **Building the Lawyer-Client Relationship**     **1**
Introduction     1
The Missouri Motivational Study     1
Setting the Stage     2

CHAPTER **2**     **Preparing the Bill**     **17**
Avoid Fee-Schedule Mentality     17
Establish Rates for Staff and Machines     18
Budgeting and Billing     20

CHAPTER **3**     **Communicating Value**     **23**
Project Effort on Paper     23
Project Honesty, Legal Ethics, and Competence     30
Project Fairness     31
Format the Bill Appropriately     32
Draft an Inviting Statement     33
Make the Bill Complete     35

CHAPTER **4**     **Employing Other Techniques that Project Effort**     **39**
Copy the Client on All Key Matters     39
Give the Client Undivided Attention in All Meetings     40
Keep Good Records of Completed Work     40
Use a Timekeeping System     40

CHAPTER **5**     **Putting the Commandments on Drafting Bills into Action**     **45**
A Summary of Highly Effective Techniques     45
Why Clients Return to You     47

POSTSCRIPT     **Fran Shellenberger**     **49**

**About the Authors**     **53**

APPENDIX A     **ABA Model Rule 1.5 of Professional Conduct**     **55**

APPENDIX B     **Resources for Choosing Time and Billing Software**     **59**

**Index**     **61**

# CHAPTER 1
# Building the Lawyer-Client Relationship

## INTRODUCTION

For the past 30 years I have written about and lectured on the topic of client relations. As a partner in a small practice, I have had the opportunity over those years to use all the tips I have offered to other lawyers. However, none of the advice I have given lawyers has had such a dramatic and immediate impact on successful client relations as my approach to drafting bills. I know that clients will rush to pay bills drafted with this approach, because it has worked for me and countless others who have motivated clients to pay bills with a high degree of reliability.

This book focuses on drafting bills that clients will understand, find justified, and hence be more likely to pay promptly than the typical lawyer's bill. Samples are provided throughout that you can use as a basis for redesigning your firm's bills. By drafting bills based on my suggested guidelines, you will better serve your clients and yourself.

The bill is a powerful vehicle for projecting the lawyer's efforts. The client wants to know what work the lawyer has done. As lawyers who wish to be paid for our hard work, we need to draft client-oriented fee statements that clients will want to pay. The bill must reflect the full scope of the effort made by all members of the legal services delivery team on the client's behalf. Consider the bill the climax of the lawyer-client relationship—its power to build or destroy that relationship should not be underestimated. If the client feels that the bill is unfair or unjustified, the client will refuse to pay it, in whole or in part; or the client may pay the bill but not recommend you to others, so you risk losing that client *and* potential referrals—a lose-lose situation.

## THE MISSOURI MOTIVATIONAL STUDY

As far back as 1960, the Prentice-Hall Missouri Motivational Study examined clients' motivations in retaining legal services. The study asked clients, the people who pay us, what they considered the most important single element that a lawyer should consider in billing for services. There were no prompts in the study format. Participants simply wrote down the 10 items they considered to be most important. Survey results revealed the following:

- 47 percent of the respondents listed effort as the most important single element in setting a fee and creating a bill
- Only 18 percent mentioned the complexity and importance of the case involved
- None of the clients surveyed even mentioned "the fee charged"
- Only 15 percent mentioned ability to pay (which lawyers have been accused of finding of great importance)
- Only 6 percent of those surveyed listed the results achieved by the lawyer

The clients said that effort is the most important element in a lawyer's bill! No subsequent research has disproved this conclusion.

Therefore, in each sample bill you will see in this book, the recommended final format includes having the amount of the bill placed between a detailed description of the work product and some individual comment. The client is not primarily interested in the amount of the bill, but rather, in the projection of EFFORT. By interlacing the amount of the bill between the description of the work done and the final comment, the amount of the bill is not given undue emphasis. A client may not even read a bill that focuses only on the amount owing. But a bill that primarily emphasizes the work that has been done will be read by the client—after all, it tells the client's story. By getting the client to read the bill—and even to look forward to receiving future bills—you increase your chances of having it paid.

Before concentrating on the kinds of bills that clients rush to pay, however, it is important to focus on the initial activities that set the stage for successful billing.

## SETTING THE STAGE

While the main focus of this book is on the actual content of the bill and style, there are activities that the lawyer engages in before and during the course of legal service that help set the stage for bills clients rush to pay. These activities include the initial client intake, first discussion of fees, fee estimate, fee agreement, and sustained client communications.

When initially thinking about a fee, consider that the client wants, in order of priority,

1. Concern
2. Honesty and Ethics
3. Competence
4. Efficiency

Thus, lawyers who place the strongest emphasis on efficiency fail to understand the client's perspective. Nonetheless, most lawyers' priorities for delivery of legal services differ from those of clients. Most lawyers' priorities are:

1. Efficiency
2. Fair fee
3. Competence
4. Concern

The Missouri Motivational Study showed that there is less than a 20 percent overlap between what lawyers and clients want out of the lawyer-client relationship. However, now that we know what clients want, and in what priority, we can be more responsive.

**The First Meeting**

As you begin the first conversation with the potential client, show that you really care. Start by expressing concern for the client, not by discussing fees. For instance, if someone tells you they have been injured, take care to show you really care about the client first as a human being. The effort projected in the bill is part of an overall approach of demonstrating concern for the client's well-being and needs, which begins at the initial intake and carries through to the final bill.

Demonstrate a high level of integrity in the way you handle cases. This will indicate to clients that there also is integrity in the billing process. Before you discuss money at the first interview, project integrity and build trust. For example, give clients some understanding about conflicts by checking for problems while clients are in your office. Then talk about their case and give an honest assessment of it before you decide whether to handle the matter. Clients should know what the lawyer's expectations are, and the lawyer must know how to manage client expectations regarding services, outcome, and billing.

Communicate competence by using the appropriate terminology, citing relevant cases you have handled or reviewed and their outcomes, and acknowledging up front some of the obstacles that you may encounter and how they can be handled. Demonstrate concern and honesty by referring the client to another lawyer when you lack competence in the subject matter to handle the case.

**Timing Fee Discussions**

The *timing* of fee discussions, billing, and payment is of vital concern to clients, and thus is important to client-oriented lawyers.

Of the Missouri study participants who said they did not use lawyers, only 1.5 percent reported that the reason was they couldn't afford the fees! (Eighty percent of the respondents in this group reported that they simply did not have a legal problem.) Among those who did use lawyers, the need for a lawyer with a *fair fee* was assigned the relatively low priority of fourth place. Finding a lawyer with a fair fee was less of a problem to the respondents than finding a lawyer who 1) was *concerned* about the client and the client's case, 2) evidenced a great respect for *ethics* and *honesty*, and 3) was *competent* to render the client service. These days, with lawyers' public image as poor as it is, it is particularly important for lawyers to be concerned about these findings.

Lawyers know that when they promise to render a legal service and a client promises to pay a fee, both parties have created a contract that will support a suit by either party. For the most part, however, clients do not care about this legal background. Experience indicates that, particularly in nonbusiness practice areas (e.g. divorces and adoptions), clients who make a substantial fee deposit up front, often with borrowed funds, simply want to know that they then have a lawyer. This all promotes the client's feeling a part of the process and experiencing greater satisfaction.

The "comfort factor" of the fee payment is highly valuable to the client. Although the law office may not have a desperate need for the fee deposit, the client has an acute need to feel sure of the employment of the lawyer. The client rests confidently in the knowledge that the lawyer is concerned and involved with the client's problems when the client has engaged the lawyer's services by paying, or promising to pay, a fee.

### Discuss the Fee

Most clients want to have at least a ballpark idea of the fee—of what it will cost them to be represented until the matter's completion. Clients, however, are afraid to raise the issue of fees with lawyers. Therefore, lawyers must initiate discussion about the cost of their services. To do so, lawyers must first assess the case, determine the time that will likely be involved, apply the rate for their time per hour, charge for staff time, and shift a pro rata share of technology costs for the case. Only then can the lawyer offer a reasonably reliable fee estimate to the client. Lawyers should overestimate the charge rather than underestimate it, as many lawyers are tempted to do to get the client's business. Remember, if you give the client an estimate that you can do the job for $5,000 and you complete it for $4,300, you're a hero. However, if you estimate a fee range of $250 to $750 and the final bill is $800, the client will be reluctant to pay.

You must have a rule that you will never let a client leave the first interview without discussing fees. Give a ballpark determination of the fee, such as, "I believe the fee will be about $500," or, "My experience is that this type of matter can normally be handled here for about $6,000." Because you will have talked about money, it means that you will keep adequate records, through which you can keep track of what your overhead is and what you ought to be charging. The client will be happy to pay you.

Of the Missouri study participants who used lawyers' services, 80 percent preferred that lawyers discuss fees in the first interview; but nearly 36 percent of the lawyers in the study did not do so. A full 92 percent of participating clients said they did not want lawyers to wait until services were completed before discussing fees; 88 percent didn't want lawyers to make the clients ask about the fees. This means that we have to readjust our thinking and be willing to discuss the fee near the end of *every* first client conference, as soon as we know what the retainer arrangements will be. Of all the disciplines that are recommended as a result of the Missouri Motivational Study findings, I know of none that requires a stronger backbone than the discussion of fees.

I have found, without exception, that discussing fees with wealthier clients near the end of the first conference places you in a businesslike position with them. They are delighted to discuss money, and they are more accustomed to professionals showing little concern for how money is spent in delivering value. This is particularly true of corporate clients, who sometimes wonder whether your rates will ultimately always exceed their budget. The first discussion puts it all on the table, up front. Further, if they don't want to pay you, can you think of a better time to find out than in the course of the initial intake?

I practice in the same community where my family has lived since the Civil War. So, as one might suspect, my firm does a considerable probate business. The great temptation for people who have known you all your life is to think that you will make an exception in their case. Eighty percent want to talk about money, and there is no more important time for discussing money than at the end of the initial meeting.

Clients need to know at the outset what your policy on billing for services is if you will give them a "deal" or treat them as you do all your clients by charging a fair fee.

The fee discussion and initial estimate lay the groundwork for a successful billing experience. Most clients want to be proud of what they're paying—and do not want any surprises when it comes to their bill. So avoid unpleasant surprises and increase your chances of being paid in full (and avoiding ethics complaints) by simply keeping the client apprised of any changes to the estimate.

Lawyers are well-advised to recognize that while they may define effort as time spent, clients do not. Most clients equate effort with service rendered, not with time. In one Texas Bar study lawyers and clients were asked how lawyers were to determine a reasonable charge. Fifty-six percent of lawyers replied, "time, or by the hour"—but only 20.4 percent of clients gave this response. The clients felt that lawyers should determine a fee based on service delivered.

Clients think of time as minutes on a clock, unrelated to service rendered or work completed. This means that clients believe a lawyer can work very hard *or* very little in an hour. Clock time is not effort in the clients' eyes. From the client's point of view, how hard the lawyer tries—as perceived by the client—is effort, and that projected effort is the service the client seeks from the legal professional. The implication of both the Texas and Missouri research is that, for most clients, bills need not include the number of hours expended but, rather, should give a detailed, specific delineation of the work completed for the client. Time expended can be detailed in a separate accounting statement and furnished upon request of the client. In addition, maintaining this time accounting is critical for proving up attorneys' fees requests made to the court. Figure 1.1 shows a bill that delineates specific work done for the client as well as a corresponding hourly time accounting statement. This is the conventional style of bill and I do not recommend it. Figure 1.2 shows a bill that delineates specific work done for the client but does not include the corresponding hourly time accounting sheet. This is the narrative and recommended style of bill.

Part of the fee may be paid into a trust account against which the lawyer draws as the work progresses. The payment of "startup funds" in the beginning representation makes the client a co-owner in the process and its outcome.

Discuss fees with every client near the end of the first interview. This is the second most important concept in projecting effort into bill drafting, behind sending clients copies of everything that pertains to the matter (discussed in Chapter 4).

### Present a Written Estimate

Always present the fee estimate in writing. If you seem to be getting close to exceeding the estimate, you should update the estimate for the client as it changes or you will be less likely to get paid. Telling someone it will cost $500 and then trying to charge them $2,000 does not show respect.

You might say, "John, remember I told you that this would cost $500. I am sorry, but I have to tell you it will cost closer to $2,000 because of...which I could never have foreseen." Keeping the client informed of fee changes is an integral part of any successful billing process. Of course, all costs exceeding a predetermined amount will require the client's preapproval.

### Utilize a Fee Agreement

A survey of grievances filed against lawyers indicates an inordinate number of such complaints come from clients who did not make fee payments in the beginning. It is well-known that clients who are not given the benefit of an up-front fee agreement do not want to pay the lawyer's bill for the service at the end of the case. I find that clients' satisfaction soars when they are given a written fee estimate that includes a written explanation of how the fee will ultimately be determined as well as a provision of up-front money.

Joe Roehl, of Albuquerque, New Mexico, conducted research some years ago with 100 law firms to determine the best time to present a final bill for legal services. He found that a final bill should be placed in the mail to the client approximately 72 hours after the

**Figure 1.1  Bill Delineating Specific Work and Accompanied by Hourly Time Statement (Conventional Style)**

Law Offices of Derby & Jackson
100 Main St.
Appleton, Texas 75432
Ph. 903-725-1000
Fax 903-725-1001

Billing timekeeper Richard J. Derby
date of last bill
date of last reminder
last bill through date
bill type code          S-1
action to be taken

| | | |
|---|---|---|
| 0 = no bill | 0 = summary only | |
| 1 = air reminder | 4 = full detail | |
| 2 = expense only bill | 5 = summary | |

October 30, 1992

Billed through 10/26/92

Bill number 22078RJD

| | |
|---|---|
| current | .00 |
| 30 days | .00 |
| 60 days | .00 |
| 90 days | .00 |
| 120 days | .00 |

Jon Town Estate
c/o Julie Barnett
Galion, Michigan County, Texas
    billing realization

billing frequency M-01
last payment
0%
fees billed to date          .00%
903-725-1004

Probate/Jon Town Estate

matter 00000

| FOR PROFESSIONAL SERVICES RENDERED | tmkp | date | hours | rate | amount |
|---|---|---|---|---|---|
| 03/16/92 Conferred with daughters and worked out filing application to probate and for appointment of successor guardian; Worked on application; Drafted order and agent for service appointment. | RJD | 03/16/92 | 3.50 | 100 | 350.00 |
| 03/16/92 Prepared check; Printed documents. | SC | 03/16/92 | .60 | 40 | 24.00 |
| 03/17/92 Prepared permanent file. | OLM | 03/17/92 | .30 | 30 | 9.00 |
| 03/17/92 Notarized application. | OLM | 03/17/92 | .10 | 30 | 3.00 |
| 03/18/92 Conferred with Julie Barnett; Will set up bank accounts at Appleton Bank tomorrow. | RJD | 03/18/92 | .30 | 100 | 30.00 |
| 03/19/92 Went to bank and secured two accounts for estates. | RJD | 03/19/92 | 1.00 | 100 | 100.00 |
| 03/23/92 Kemper IRA account should be cashed and deposited into estate account. | RJD | 03/23/92 | .30 | 100 | 30.00 |
| 03/31/92 Appeared in court, made proof of death and secured order probating will. | RJD | 03/31/92 | .40 | 100 | 40.00 |
| 03/31/92 Telephoned Doris re: letters testamentary. | JBW | 03/31/92 | .10 | 40 | 4.00 |
| 04/01/92 Conferred with client and bank to work out accounts that comport with probate orders. | RJD | 04/01/92 | 1.00 | 100 | 100.00 |
| 04/01/92 Delivered letter to Appleton Bank. | JBW | 04/01/92 | .40 | 40 | 16.00 |
| 04/02/92 Prepared letter to client. | JBW | 04/02/92 | .40 | 40 | 16.00 |
| 04/06/92 Conferred with Julie Barnett concerning account expenditures. | RJD | 04/06/92 | .30 | 100 | 30.00 |

| 04/13/92 | Returned call to Julie Barnett; Called bank and checked on account. | RJD | 04/13/92 | 1.00 | 100 | 100.00 |
|---|---|---|---|---|---|---|
| 04/13/92 | Prepared letter to Harald Times with copy to client. Prepared notice. | SC | 04/13/92 | .60 | 40 | 24.00 |
| 05/14/92 | Prepared letter to client. | JBW | 05/14/92 | .50 | 40 | 20.00 |
| 05/21/92 | Returned call from Julie Barnett; Learned income payments have been received— Aetna $7,500.00; Campus Life Ins. $5,000; Investor Life of Nevada $7,657. No active 91 policy; Learned Julie will be here June 11 and 12; She will be available the week of June 15. | RJD | 05/21/92 | .20 | 100 | 20.00 |
| 05/27/92 | Printed inventory, appraisement and list of claims and began to prepare Schedule C. | SC | 05/27/92 | 2.00 | 40 | 80.00 |
| 05/28/92 | Completed Schedule C and prepared a letter to clients and memo to Mr. Derby. | SC | 05/28/92 | 3.00 | 40 | 120.00 |
| 06/18/92 | Worked on accounting. | RJD | 06/18/92 | .50 | 100 | 50.00 |
| 06/23/92 | Worked on inventory in all estates. | | 06/23/92 | 2.00 | 100 | 200.00 |
| 07/01/92 | Contacted bank with executor in effort to arrange the loan. | RJD | 07/01/92 | 1.00 | 100 | 100.00 |
| 07/10/92 | Researched library forms; Crafted and printed Order Approving Final Accounting. | ADD | 07/10/92 | 1.40 | 40 | 56.00 |
| 07/13/92 | Went to courthouse and researched court jacket—checking to see if final accounting had been approved. | ADD | 07/13/92 | .30 | 40 | 12.00 |
| 07/15/92 | Send file stamped Order Approving Account for final settlement to client; cover letter. | OLM | 07/15/92 | .20 | 30 | 6.00 |
| 08/17/92 | Conference with RJD; Located documents to file; Prepared Application for Sale of Real Property; Prepared Order setting Hearing on Application; Prepared Order of Sale of Real Property; Prepared Decree Confirming Sale; Prepared Deed for Sale. Reviewed probate code; Memo to RJD; Telephone call to Hunt County Appraisal District; Returned call to Smith Title (twice); Drafted application for guardianship; Prepared Verified Exhibits A & B. | ADC | 08/17/92 | 5.50 | 40 | 220.00 |
| 08/17/92 | Telephone call to Joan at Smith Title for terms of sale of home; Revised application; Submitted to RJD. | ADC | 08/17/92 | .50 | 40 | 20.00 |
| 08/19/92 | Conference with RJD; Reviewed probate code; Telephone call from Julie Barnett; Obtained fax number; Revised application and exhibits and printed; Prepared fax cover sheet; Fax to Julie Barnett; Refaxed revised Exhibit B; Faxed to Julie Barnett; Prepared for filing; Telephone call to clerk's office regarding costs; Copied all documents; Prepared check. | ADC | 08/19/92 | 2.60 | 40 | 104.00 |
| 08/20/92 | Revised Order of Sale of Real Property; Copied document; Filed document at courthouse; Memo to file; Letter to Julie Barnett with copy of document. | ADC | 08/20/92 | .90 | 40 | 36.00 |

| 09/03/92 | Prepared letter to J. Barnett enclosing Order Setting Hearing. | ADC | 09/03/92 | .10 | 40 | 4.00 |
|---|---|---|---|---|---|---|
| 09/03/92 | Prepared checks for Order Approving Sale of Real Property and for Order Setting Hearing on application; Entered orders at Clerk's office; Reviewed code for next step; Telephoned Joan at Smith Title; Telephone from Joan. | ADC | 09/03/92 | .80 | 40 | 32.00 |
| 09/03/92 | Telephoned Joan at Smith Title re: status of file. | ADC | 09/03/92 | .40 | 40 | 16.00 |
| 09/09/92 | Located probate file; Conferred with Tracy; Reviewed and copied Section 341 of Probate Code; Prepared memo to file. | ADC | 09/09/92 | .30 | 40 | 12.00 |
| 09/14/92 | Telephoned Joan at Smith Title re: faxing copy. | ADC | 09/14/92 | .10 | 40 | 4.00 |
| 09/15/92 | Telephone with Joan at Smith Title re: order signed; Revised Report of Sale printed; Copied exhibits to attach; Conferred with RJD. | ADC | 09/15/92 | .50 | 40 | 20.00 |
| 09/18/92 | Revised Report of Sale; Prepared Federal Express to Julie Barnett; Conference with RJD. | ADC | 09/18/92 | .90 | 40 | 36.00 |
| 09/21/92 | Prepared decree confirming sale; Copied documents for courthouse; Prepared check for filing; To courthouse and filed Decree Conf. Sale and Rep. of Sale. | ADC | 09/21/92 | .90 | 40 | 36.00 |
| 09/25/92 | Telephone from Julie Barnett re: send letter-testamentary to brother at 124 Wolcott, Dallas, TX 75240; Telephone to Clerk's office re: preparing letters; Revised deed; Prepared letter to Jon, Jr. | ADC | 09/25/92 | .70 | 40 | 28.00 |
| 10/07/92 | Telephone from Smith Title re: tax ID numbers; Telephoned Julie Barnett, left message;Telephone from Julie Barnett; Telephoned Smith Title. | ADC | 10/07/92 | .40 | 40 | 16.00 |
| | $2,124.00 | | | | 36.00 | 2124.00 |

DISBURSEMENTS

| | | | | | |
|---|---|---|---|---|---|
| Filing fees—Hunt County Clerk for Application for Probate of Will and Issuance of Letters Testamentary | 128.25 | 150 | 03/16/92 | | 128.25 |
| Filing fees—Hunt County Clerk for Application for Guardian | 12.00 | 150 | 03/17/92 | | 12.00 |
| Hunt County Clerk for Letters of Guardianship | 20.00 | 99 | 03/24/92 | | 20.00 |
| Hunt County Clerk for Letters of Testamentary | 12.00 | 99 | 03/31/92 | | 12.00 |
| Long distance | .33 | 116 | 04/01/92 | | .33 |
| Long distance | 1.10 | 117 | 04/02/92 | | 1.10 |

| | | | | | |
|---|---|---|---|---|---|
| Postage | .29 | 110 | 04/03/92 | | .29 |
| Long distance | 1.33 | 116 | 04/13/92 | | 1.33 |
| Long distance | .31 | 116 | 04/13/92 | | .31 |
| Postage | .58 | 110 | 04/13/92 | | .52 |
| Postage | .52 | 110 | 05/01/92 | | .52 |
| Postage | .29 | 110 | 05/14/92 | | .29 |
| Appleton Herald Times | 48.54 | 99 | 05/20/92 | | 48.54 |
| Long distance | 1.28 | 116 | 05/21/92 | | 1.28 |
| Barnes & Haynes | 252.96 | 99 | 05/21/92 | | 252.96 |
| Hunt County Clerk for Letters of Testamentary | 2.00 | 99 | 06/30/92 | | 2.00 |
| Filing fees—Hunt County Clerk | 58.00 | 150 | 07/02/92 | | 58.00 |
| Copying | .30 | 100 | 07/10/92 | | .30 |
| Hunt County Clerk | 5.00 | 99 | 07/13/92 | | 5.00 |
| Postage | .29 | 110 | 07/15/92 | | .29 |
| Filing fees—Hunt County Clerk for Application for Sale of Real Property | 56.00 | 150 | 08/19/92 | | 56.00 |
| Fax transmittal | 18.00 | 180 | 08/19/92 | | 18.00 |
| Fax transmittal | 9.00 | 180 | 08/19/92 | | 9.00 |
| Copying | 6.00 | 100 | 08/20/92 | | 6.00 |
| Copying | 1.65 | 100 | 08/20/92 | | 1.65 |
| Postage | .52 | 110 | 08/20/92 | | .52 |
| Postage | .29 | 110 | 09/03/92 | | .29 |
| Hunt County Clerk for order setting hearing on Application | 8.00 | 99 | 09/03/92 | | 8.00 |
| Copying | .60 | 100 | 09/08/92 | | .60 |
| Fax transmittal | 15.00 | 180 | 09/14/92 | | 15.00 |
| Court costs—Hunt County Clerk for order | 18.00 | 130 | 09/21/92 | | 18.00 |
| Hunt County Clerk for Letters of Testamentary | 4.00 | 99 | 09/25/92 | | 4.00 |
| Copying | .15 | 100 | 09/25/92 | | .15 |
| Postage | .29 | 110 | 09/25/92 | | .29 |
| Long distance | .67 | 117 | 10/07/92 | | .67 |
| Federal Express | 13.00 | 99 | 10/09/92 | | 13.00 |
| | $696.54 | | | | 696.54 |

BILLING SUMMARY

| | | | | |
|---|---|---|---|---|
| | | SC | 6.20 | 40 | 248.00 |
| | | ADC | 16.30 | 40 | 652.00 |
| | | CLM | .60 | 30 | 18.00 |
| | | RJD | 11.50 | 100 | 1150.00 |
| | | JBW | 1.40 | 40 | 56.00 |

| | | | | |
|---|---|---|---|---|
| TOTAL FEES | $2,124.00 | | 36.00 | 2,124.00 |
| TOTAL DISBURSEMENTS | $696.54 | | | 696.54 |
| TOTAL CHARGES FOR THIS BILL | $2,820.54 | | | 2,820.54 |

**Figure 1.2**     **Bill Delineating Effort (Narrative Style)**

Law Offices of Derby & Jackson
100 Main St.
Appleton, Texas 75432
Ph. 903-725-1000   Fax 903-725-1001
October 30, 1992
Billed through 10/26/92
Bill number 22078RJD

Jon Town Estate
c/o Julie Barnett
Galion, Michigan County, Texas

Probate/Jon Town Estate

Balance forward                                                    $ 0.00

FOR PROFESSIONAL SERVICES RENDERED

03/16/92—Conferred with daughters and worked out filing application to probate and for appointment of successor guardian; Worked on application; Drafted order and agent for service appointment; Prepared check; Printed documents; 03/17/92—Prepared permanent file; Notarized application; 03/18/92—Conferred with Julie Barnett; Planned establishment of two accounts at Appleton Bank tomorrow; 03/19/92—Went to bank and secured two accounts for estates; 03/23/92—Confirmed Kemper IRA account cashed and deposited into estate account; 03/31/92—Appeared in court, made proof of death and secured order probating will; Telephoned Doris re: letters testementary; 04/01/92—Conferred with client and bank to work out accounts that comport with probate orders; Delivered letter to Appleton bank; 04/02/92—Prepared letter to client; 04/06/92—Conferred with Julie Barnett concerning account expenditures; 04/13/92—Returned call to Julie Barnett; Called bank and checked on account; Prepared letter to Harald Times with copy to client; Prepared notice; 05/14/92—Prepared letter to client; 05/21/92—Returned call from Julie Barnett; Learned income payment have been received as follows: Aetna $7,500.00; Campus Life Ins. $5,000; Investor Life of Nevada $7,657. No active 91 policy; 05/27/92—Printed inventory, appraisement, and list of claims and began to prepare Schedule C; 05/28/92—Completed Schedule C and prepared a letter to clients and memo to Mr. Derby; 06/18/92—Worked on accounting; 06/23/92—Worked on inventory in all estates; 07/01/92—Contacted bank with executor in effort to arrange the loan; 07/10/92—Researched library forms; Crafted and printed Order Approving Final Accounting; 07/13/92—Went to courthouse and researched court jacket, checking for approval of final accounting; 07/15/92—Sent file stamped Order Approving Account for final settlement to client; cover letter; 08/17/92—Conference with RJD; Located documents to file; Prepared Application for Sale of Real Property; Prepared Order setting Hearing on Application; Prepared Order of Sale of Real Property; Prepared Decree Confirming Sale; Prepared Deed for Sale. Reviewed probate code; Memo to RJD; Telephone call to Hunt County Appraisal District; Returned call to Smith Title (twice); Drafted application for guardianship; Prepared Verified Exhibits A & B; 08/17/92—Telephone call to Joan at Smith Title for terms of sale of home; Revised application; Submitted to RJD; 08/19/92—Conference with RJD; Reviewed probate code; Telephone call from Julie Barnett; Obtained fax number; Revised application and

Jon Town Estate
Bill number 22078RJD                                               Page 2

exhibits and printed; Prepared fax cover sheet; Fax to Julie Barnett; Refaxed revised Exhibit B; Prepared for filing; Telephone call to clerk's office regarding costs; Copied all documents; Prepared check; 08/20/92—Revised Order of Sale of Real Property; Copied documents; Filed document at courthouse; Memo to file; Letter to Julie Barnett with copy of document; 09/03/92—Prepared letter to Julie Barnett enclosing Order Setting Hearing; 09/03/92—Prepared checks for Order Approving Sale of Real Property and for Order Setting Hearing on application; Entered orders at Clerk's office; Reviewed code for next step; Telephoned Joan at Smith Title re: status of file; 09/09/92—Located probate file; Conferred with Tracy; Reviewed and copied Section 341 of Probate Code; Prepared memo to file; 09/14/92—Telephoned Joan at Smith Title re: faxing copy; 09/15/92—Telephone with Joan at Smith Title re: order signed; Revised Report of Sale printed; Copied exhibits to attach; Conferred with RJD; 09/18/92—Revised Report of Sale; Prepared Federal Express to Julie Barnett; Conferred with RJD; 09/21/92—Prepared decree confirming sale; Copied documents for courthouse; Prepared check for filing; To courthouse and filed Decree Conf. Sale and Rep. of Sale; 09/25/92—Telephone form Julie Barnett re: send letter-testementary to brother at 124 Wolcott, Dallas, TX 75240; Telephone to Clerk's office re: preparing letters; Revised deed; Prepared letter to Jon, Jr.; 10/09/92—Telephone from Smith Title re: tax ID numbers; Telephoned Julie Barnett, left message; Telephone from Julie Barnett; Telephoned Smith Title.

$2,124.00

DISBURSEMENTS

| | |
|---|---:|
| Filing fees—Hunt County Clerk Application for Probate of Will and Issuance of Letters Testamentary | 128.25 |
| Filing fees—Hunt County Clerk for Application for Guardian | 12.00 |
| Hunt County Clerk for Letters of Guardianship | 20.00 |
| Hunt County Clerk for Letters of Testamentary | 12.00 |
| Long distance | .33 |
| Long distance | 1.10 |
| Postage | .29 |
| Long distance | 1.33 |
| Long distance | .31 |
| Postage | .52 |
| Postage | .52 |
| Postage | .29 |
| Appleton Herald Times | 48.54 |
| Long distance | 1.28 |
| Barnes & Haynes | 252.96 |

Jon Town Estate
Bill number 22078RJD                                      Page 3

| | |
|---|---:|
| Hunt County Clerk for Letters of Testamentary | 2.00 |
| Filing fees—Hunt County Clerk | 58.00 |
| Copying | .30 |
| Hunt County Clerk | 5.00 |
| Postage | .29 |
| Filing fees—Hunt County Clerk for Application for Sale of Real Property | 56.00 |
| Fax transmittal | 18.00 |
| Fax transmittal | 9.00 |
| Copying | 6.00 |
| Copying | 1.65 |
| Postage | .52 |
| Postage | .29 |
| Hunt County Clerk for order setting hearing on Application | 8.00 |
| Copying | .60 |
| Fax transmittal | 15.00 |
| Court costs—Hunt County Clerk for order | 18.00 |
| Hunt County Clerk for Letters of Testamentary | 4.00 |
| Copying | .15 |
| Postage | .29 |
| Long distance | .67 |
| Federal Express | 13.00 |
| | $696.54 |

BILLING SUMMARY

| | |
|---|---:|
| TOTAL FEES | 2,124.00 |
| TOTAL DISBURSEMENTS | $696.54 |
| TOTAL CHARGES FOR THIS BILL | $2,820.54 |
| TOTAL CHARGES NOW DUE | $2,820.54 |

Thank you very much for your confidence in our firm. Your record-keeping practices greatly assisted us in rendering our services in behalf of your father's estate.

work on the case or matter has been completed. As in the Missouri study, the Roehl finding evidences that a businesslike attitude on the part of a lawyer is a major factor in a client's decision to re-engage the lawyer for additional work. Being "businesslike" includes discussing and handling financial issues up front.

When I bill clients at the intervals agreed on, I project the businesslike attitude that is so important to clients. Billing a client when the law firm needs cash flow or the lawyer has some extra time is not businesslike—it is unprofessional. In building and maintaining law practices in these highly competitive times, none of us is so client-oriented by birth or training that he or she cannot benefit from taking a regular inventory of client-oriented skills.

Try to have a fee agreement up-front for all cases. The fee agreement should be a standard form, prepared prior to the first client meeting. This is much easier to get clients to accept. It is more palatable for most clients to know that you are asking them to sign the same form that you use for all other clients. Thus they do not feel singled out for possibly less favorable treatment.

Write in the service to be performed, the hourly rate depending on the situation, and all costs the client will be expected to cover, including those for legal assistants' time, research, fax charges, machine time, etc. Electronic research is generally charged back just like machine time. For billing purposes, you can account for long-distance calls via a tracking system offered by most telephone companies. This system allows you to track and time outgoing calls by case number as you dial the telephone number. Photocopies can be accounted for by counters based on case number as well. Techniques like these lend greater credibility to the bill. Explain all these tracking systems in the first meeting so that the client realizes how much integrity is built into your cost-allocation process.

Bear in mind that what you want is an *agreement* with the client, not a formal contract. Otherwise clients will need a lawyer to review their lawyer contracts. Therefore, avoid semantic double talk—it's essential that the agreement be easy to read and understand. A sample fee agreement is shown in Figure 1.3.

In those practice areas where fees are determined by statute, there is no need for a fee agreement. Nonetheless, it is still essential to give the client a verbal estimate and then to keep accurate time records.

**FIGURE 1.3**      **Agreement for Legal Services**

The Law Office of Green & Roberts agrees to provide legal services in the
_____

matter discussed by the undersigned attorney and client and the client agrees to pay the following:

It is understood that attorney time will be billed at the rate of $_____ per hour, with support staff, including legal assistant functions, at rates from $_____ to $_____ per hour plus machine time, systems use, electronic research, and fax charges. In the event travel is necessary, mileage is billed at the rate of $_____ per mile. Xerox copies are billed at the rate of $_____ per copy. All long-distance telephone calls will be charged to the client.

Responsibility to provide legal services will be accepted and work will begin when we receive $_____ as a minimum retainer against attorney's fees and expenses.

Client agrees to reimburse attorneys for expenses incurred on client's behalf, including court costs, deposition expense, services and testimony of expert witnesses and investigators, and other discovery procedures. Attorneys will not obligate client for any large expense in excess of $_____ without client's prior approval.

If and when it becomes apparent that the above amounts for fees and expenses will be expended under this agreement, an additional sum will be set by attorneys.

Client agrees that attorney's fees and expenses shall become due and payable upon receipt of a statement for services rendered and expenses incurred. As a condition of employment, client agrees that attorneys have the right to cease legal work and keep all funds received for legal work services if client does not make additional deposits as requested by attorneys.

Client understands and agrees that the fees which client agrees to pay under this contract do not apply to any further litigation after judgment is entered. This agreement does not include legal services on appeal. In the event an appeal is determined to be necessary after trial, a new agreement will be negotiated.

Any sums collected from client's opposing party will be credited against client's obligation, but only when actually received by attorneys.

Client understands and agrees that attorneys make no promises or guarantees as to the outcome of the case other than to provide client with reasonable and necessary legal services.

This agreement is performable in <u>City</u>, <u>County</u>, <u>State</u>.

Each of the undersigned has read the above agreement and agrees to each of the terms and conditions stated above.

SIGNED this _____ day of _____, 19_____.

Law Offices of Green & Roberts

_____          By: _____

Client                                               Attorney

# CHAPTER **II**
# **Preparing the Bill**

Component billing is a practical approach to pricing the services of legal services delivery teams. For example, a bill can include charges for the use of an electronic forms library, which, in essence, is a charge for the development of a computer system.

The technological revolution—including computers, substantive law systems, document assembly systems, fax machines, modems, and well-trained support staff—is forcing lawyers to rethink how a fair fee for legal services should be determined.

We must continue to redefine what we mean by value. However, this is the subject of other books, specifically *Win-Win Billing Strategies* and *Beyond the Billable Hour: An Anthology of Alternative Billing Methods,* both published by the ABA Section of Law Practice Management.

## AVOID FEE-SCHEDULE MENTALITY

Lawyers once relied upon mandatory fee schedules—ruled unconstitutional by the U.S. Supreme Court in 1975. Many firms continue to utilize internal voluntary fee schedules. In our firm, we discovered that if you always rely upon a fee schedule, you may starve to death. We found that those who only sometimes consulted the fee schedule at our firm made more than 10 percent more money—and those who ignored the schedule entirely made a good 25 percent more.

If your firm uses fee schedule guidelines to tell lawyers how to bill, make certain they have been developed analytically—based on time and motion studies and, to some extent, weighted for the responsibilities that different partners, associates, and nonlawyers bear. That is to say, unless a fee schedule is based on the actual cost of providing legal services, be cautious in using it as a basis of your billing, as it will more often than not undercompensate.

We know that people do not seek an initial consultation merely because they are shopping around and pricing you. Potential clients are looking for a basis of confidence, friendliness, promptness, businesslike manner, and courtesy. They choose us more on the basis of services we have rendered that they have heard reports about—much more than any perceived bargain our fee estimate suggests.

## ESTABLISH RATES FOR STAFF AND MACHINES

A staff member is not an overhead burden, but a part of the team that produces the fee. After careful analysis, many offices will find they are best served by assigning a charge to a given service a staff person renders. What rate should be assigned to each staff person? Start by establishing a rate calculated to produce billings at three times salary and fringe benefits, just as law firms have done for associates.

The word processor who types a case document or runs spreadsheets for case analysis has an annual salary, works a number of hours, and has a billing rate, and these factors help determine the value of the service to the client.

First, consider that many smaller law offices are open for business only 1,948 hours per year. With vacations, sick leave, and funerals, the number of chargeable hours is reduced by at least 160, representing one month lost. This leaves 1,780 hours per year, or a little over 160 hours for each of the 11 months actually worked. Reduce that amount by 25 percent, or 445 hours, which represents the "fudge factor" for time that will not get recorded. This leaves 1,335 hours per year, which is about 120 hours per month, or 30 hours per week for the months worked.

If you use a staff member with a $16,000 yearly salary, the cost per hour to the firm is 1,335 divided into $16,000, which is $11.99, rounded to $12 per hour. The billing rate for this staff member at the conservative three-times multiplier (salary + overhead + profit) is $36 per hour. If four times salary is used, the billing rate is $48.

Begin by determining how many calls are received by the receptionist each day. Actual records usually produce evidence of twice the number of calls originally estimated. In a three-person law firm the number of calls per week may exceed 250, which is more than 1,000 per month, or 11,000 calls for the work year. If the receptionist earns $16,000 annually and answers the phones full-time, each call costs the firm $1.45. Three times the raw cost is $4.35 and is usually rounded off for a client charge of $5 per call.

Machines also do legal work and need a rate assigned. While staff services are charged at rates three times salaries and fringes, machines are best charged at two times (overhead + profit) actual cost.

Some machine charges are already a part of the customary billing procedure in most law offices and require no radical change in handling. Charges for metered postage and photocopies, for example, are listed as reimbursable expenses on most client statements. Most firms show the cost of copies at a higher charge than the raw cost, and the procedure requires no change. The customary charge of 10 to 25 cents per copy represents a recovery of roughly twice the raw cost to the firm, which ranges from 7 to 10 cents per page depending on equipment.

Computers and printers are best charged through a rate charge per printed page. Four computers, with word processing software, tied to a single laser printer represent a firm investment of about $10,000. The life of the equipment is probably three years. In a small law firm, the equipment may produce about 4,000 pages per month, or 48,000 pages per year, for roughly 150,000 pages over the three-year life of the equipment. Printer cartridges and equipment maintenance cost the firm about $100 per 4,000 pages of production, or 2.5¢ per page. The equipment use cost is determined by dividing the $10,000 cost by 150,000 pages (the number of pages produced over the life of the equipment). The raw cost of the equipment per page is a little over 6¢. This 6¢ plus the printing cost of 2.5¢ equal a total bare cost to the firm of 8.5¢ per page. At two times bare costs, the per-page production charge for the machines is 17¢, usually charged at 20¢ per page.

Computerized research is also a machine function and so is properly charged at two times bare cost. If the research charge for Lexis or Westlaw, for example, is $60, the client fee should be $120. This is not a reimbursable expense—it is a rightful part of the legal fee, as is an hourly rate for doing research manually.

By using component billing to determine a fair value fee for the client, law firms need not fear the cost of new technological advances. Machines are simply accepted as part of the delivery of legal services. For example, when the raw per-page cost of facsimile equipment is determined and the fee charge is twice the raw cost per page, the fax equipment becomes a part of the fee production of the firm—and not a part of the firm's overhead burden.

The critical point is that charges for machines used in producing legal services should be factored into the client billing process. Building substantive systems to produce paperwork for a divorce, a sound sale contract for nonresidential real estate, or electronic forms that eliminate the need for dictation for simple wills or contingency trusts saves valuable lawyer's time. When the system is developed and installed, it doubles, or triples, the lawyer's productivity by cutting the lawyer's time involvement by 80 percent or more.

The time spent developing these practice aids is an investment in the future of the practice, just as the purchase of a machine with a three-year useful life is an investment in that future. When a system is used for the benefit of a client, the client receives a value that must be charged for as part of the legal fee or bill.

If, for example, four hours of $125 per-hour time is used to draft and install a forms library to avoid dictation of simple wills, the firm has invested $500 in this system. If the estimated log use is 60 times during the next three years, the raw cost of each use is $8.33. Twice the raw cost is $16.66. The charge to the client's bill for the use of the log, and the resulting reduction in lawyer's time, is rounded up to $17.

Developing a form to avoid dictation in a divorce-suit property settlement may require two hours of $125 per-hour time. The firm estimates it will use this form 25 times over the next three years. Since the raw cost is $250, the raw cost per use is $10. Twice the raw cost is $20. Each time the form is used to benefit a client and reduce the lawyer's time required to provide the service, the charge of $20 is added into the determination of the fee.

The same procedure can be followed for computer software use. The raw cost of the software installed is determined, and the number of times the software will be used is estimated for a three-year period.

Thereby the raw cost to the firm for each use is determined. Again, the amount to be included in determining a proper value fee is twice the raw cost.

## BUDGETING AND BILLING

The first step in the budgeting process is determining how much it costs to run your law firm. Let's say your overhead (including staff salaries) is $75,000. The second step is determining how much you are worth on an annual basis, or, stated another way: How much net profit do you need to take home? If this figure is $100,000, then you will need to collect $175,000 in fees. Of the time that is entered into your system, however, as much as 25 percent will not be charged for, billed, or collected. Thus, you will have to add 25 percent to the fees you actually collect in order to establish a billing goal. See below:

| | |
|---|---|
| $100,000 | for you |
| +$ 75,000 | overhead (including salaries) |
| $175,000 | **Total** |
| +$ 43,750 | the 25 percent written off |
| $218,750 | **Total Billing Goal** |

In this example, the lawyer will have to charge for $218,750 in order to take home $100,000. In order to reach this billing goal, the lawyer will have to charge an average billing rate of $163.86 ($218,750 ÷ 1,335 hours). If the sum of all chargeable items (lawyer, staff, machines, etc.) does not return $163.86 per hour, the billing goal will not be reached. The shortfall, then, will come out of the lawyer's pocket.

Because the bill itself will reflect effort rather than hours, why is time important? The answer is that time is *the* major factor in determining the amount of the fee.

A proper estimate recognizes that the production of legal services is a team operation, including

● Lawyering
● Word processing
● Administration
● Delegation

Delegation is vital for the efficient production of legal services. For example, where there are written procedures and a quality staff person or legal assistant, the lawyer can delegate a substantial amount of work without the necessity for detailed supervision by the lawyer. Every person in the law firm is entitled to a billing rate. If you need to increase your gross income, it can be done in much smaller increments when everyone in the office has a billing rate. More importantly, the billing is more accurate because the client pays for the services actually rendered.

So, determine your gross expenses by the aforementioned method. Then for a given person in your office, determine how many chargeable hours that person will work in a year. Each person must produce three times what they are earning. For example,

$16,000 annual salary

x 3
_____

$48,000 **Total**

The $48,000 divided by 1,335 hours per year equals a $36 per-hour billing rate of that person.

If you utilize this component approach to billing, you will generate a chargeable amount that reaches your billing goal *and* reflects effort to the client. If the client perceives the value of your services, the payment of the fee will not be such a painful experience.

# CHAPTER **III**
# Communicating Value

## PROJECT EFFORT ON PAPER

Projecting effort on paper is a paramount consideration in designing bills that clients will rush to pay. Three basic ideas need to be mastered:

- Delineation of work done
- Verb orientation
- The "time versus service" duality

Each aspect is discussed below, accompanied by detailed sample bills that put the principles into practice.

### Delineate Work Done

The bills client clients rush to pay delineate all work done for the client and the date on which each effort was expended. A simple bill, for example, might read: "January 21, 1994, conferred with John Jones concerning limited partnership for Smally Development, with determination that general partner should be an individual rather than a corporation."

Bills should never refer simply to "briefing" or "research," but rather should describe the matter that was briefed or researched. For example, a bill that refers to "January 23, 1994, briefing in Jones and Smith matter" is weak. But the same bill drafted in a slightly different fashion, "January 23, 1994, briefing of directors' liability to minority stockholders in Jones and Smith matter," has more impact and is more acceptable to the client. By delineating the exact propositions investigated through legal research, the lawyer projects concern and intelligent effort on behalf of the client. The method is illustrated in Figure 3.1.

Bills can also refer to discussions that convey concern about individuals' viewpoints and well-being, as shown in Figure 3.2.

**Figure 3.1**          **Bill Delineating Effort**

---

Law Offices of Benton and Arth
One Chestnut Plaza
Ocean Haven, Maryland 21611
Ph. 301-988-6600   FAX 301-988-6601
August 27, 1992
Billed through 08/23/92
Bill number   21501-012 BAA

Adam Langford
168 Winchester St.
Ocean Haven, Maryland 21622

Divorce/Kimberly Langford

| | |
|---|---|
| Balance forward as of bill number 009 dated 09/25/91 | $1,086.00 |
| Payments received since last bill (last payment 10/08/92) | $1,086.00 |
| Net balance forward | $    .00 |

FOR PROFESSIONAL SERVICES RENDERED

09/23/91—Telephoned Mike Von re: decree; Left message with Debbie; 09/25/91—Telephone from Mike Von re: decree, he hasn't completed it yet; 10/02/91—Telephoned Von re: decree, he said it will be ready in a week; 10/10/91—Telephoned Von re: decree, left message; 10/14/91—Telephoned Von re: decree, left message; 10/22/91—Telephoned Von re: decree, he has prepared draft and is waiting for his client to review; 10/29/91—Telephoned Von regarding Order; 11/12/91—Conferred with client about divorce settlement order; Called Von; 11/14/91—Prepared a letter to Von by fax; 11/14/91—Drafted letter to Von about Sears problem and need for immediate order to be drafted; 01/21/92—Conferred with client; Spa is problem; Wife is to be awarded spa and she must pay for it; 01/22/92—Prepared letter to Von; 01/22/92—In court; Worked out problem with decree's placing spa to Mr. Langford when it should be to Mrs. Langford; We will need set off for money paid on debts assumed by Mrs. Langford; Drafted letter to Von with proposal; 02/18/92—Made telephone call to Von's office to determine progress on my January 22, 1992, letter to him; 03/03/92—Prepared letter to client, and enclosed proposed decree; 03/10/92—Prepared letter to client; Calendared and docketed file; 03/23/92—Telephoned Mike Von re: errors in order re: spa and cover; Left message to call BAA; 03/30/92—Appeared in court to get orders entered, but wife did not appear and court removed from docket for one week; 04/01/92—Calendared and docketed file; Prepared letter to client; Telephoned client regarding hearing; 04/13/92—Appeared in court on entry of judgment; Read transcript, but could not agree with method to put dispute aside; Determined to enter judgment as provided in statement of fact and take up negotiations after judgment is signed by court; 04/20/92—Prepared letter to client; Calendared and docketed file; 04/30/92—Appeared in court; 05/29/92—Prepared letter to client; Calendared and docketed file; 08/07/92—Mailed client copy of Nunc Pro Tunc Order.

$472.00

---

Adam Langford
Bill number 21501-012 BAA                                    Page 2


DISBURSEMENTS

| | |
|---|---:|
| Fax transmittal | 8.00 |
| Fax transmittal | 18.00 |
| Long distance | 2.03 |
| Long distance | .14 |
| Postage | .52 |
| Postage | .52 |
| Fax transmittal | 9.00 |
| Postage | .29 |
| Postage | .29 |
| Postage | .29 |
| Postage | .29 |
| Postage | .52 |
| | $39.89 |

BILLING SUMMARY

| | |
|---|---:|
| TOTAL FEES | $472.00 |
| TOTAL DISBURSEMENTS | $39.89 |
| TOTAL CHARGES FOR THIS BILL | $511.89 |
| TOTAL BALANCE NOW DUE | $511.89 |

**FIGURE 3.2**  **Bill Referencing Discussions to Convey Concern**

Law Offices of Franklin, Whitney & Behn
454 Second Ave.
Chicago, Illinois 60670
Ph. 312-996-8100   FAX 312-996-8106
February 18, 1992
Billed through 02/16/92
Bill number   22053-014  HNJ

Francis Craig
24 Glenview St.
Chicago, IL 60695

Prepaid balance brought forward                                      $500.00 CR

Divorce/Marilyn Craig

FOR PROFESSIONAL SERVICES RENDERED

01/20/92—Conferred with client concerning child and need for support from Craig's parents; 01/21/92—Prepared Original Answer and Counterclaim and Temporary Restraining Order and Order Setting Hearing; 01/21/92—Prepared permanent file; 01/21/92—Reviewed facts with client; Outlined pleadings for legal assistant; Secured signature on Oath documents from client; 01/22/92—Revised Craig Original Answer and Counterclaim and the TRO and Order Setting Hearing; 01/22/92—Telephoned to set Temporary Restraining Order; Prepared check; 01/22/92—Prepared letter to client; Calendared and docketed file; 01/22/92— Conferred with Francis Craig's parents concerning their view of case; Also approved pleadings; 01/23/92—Telephoned Mary Rodriguez in regard to service. Ms. Craig was served at approximately 9:00 a.m. today; 01/24/92—Prepared letter to client; Calendared and docketed file; 01/27/92—Conferred with client, developing facts and feelings; 01/28/92—Conferred with client about child and possible counseling; 01/29/92—Conferred with client; 02/06/92—Conferred with client and learned that his wife is hospitalized in LaGrange; 02/11/92—Prepared a letter to David Lawson returning the approved temporary order.

                                                                          $734.00

DISBURSEMENTS

| | |
|---|---:|
| Court costs - Cook County District Clerk - citation and TRO | 31.00 |
| Copying Mary Rodriguez | 11.40 |
| Court costs - services | 80.00 |
| Postage | .29 |
| Postage | .29 |
| Postage | .29 |
| | $123.27 |

BILLING SUMMARY

| | |
|---|---:|
| TOTAL FEES | $734.00 |
| TOTAL DISBURSEMENTS | $123.27 |
| TOTAL CHARGES FOR THIS BILL | $857.27 |
| LESS PREPAID AMOUNT | $500.00 |
| TOTAL BALANCE NOW DUE | $357.27 |

### Use Blocking And Punctuation To Project Effort Visually

Block billing—that is, the construction of a bill without paragraphs—is a visual means of projecting effort. Six lines in a bill, separated into three paragraphs, appear to the client as three work items. The client might automatically assume that each work item, or paragraph, represents one-third of the total fee shown. If the three paragraphs are placed together as one block, the client's visual acceptance of the work effort description is enhanced. No longer is the work effort divided into thirds; it appears as one continuous effort for which the client is happy to pay.

It is also advisable to use semicolons rather than periods to separate one work product from another, so that the eye moves from one work-effort description to the next without hesitation. Note how these concepts add to the effectiveness of Figure 3.3.

### Use Verbs To Convey Action

The bills that clients rush to pay should use many verbs, as well as verb-derived words that recount action in a "play-by-play" style. A bill that reads "January 23, 1994, loan agreement, deed of trust mortgage and note" is ineffective. It does not project effort as well as "January 23, 1994, drafted loan agreement, examined deed of trust mortgage and note." Words like "drafted," "conferred," "prepared," "examined," and "determined" appear frequently in bills that clients rush to pay. Notice the frequency of such action verbs in Figure 3.4.

### Use Smaller Billing Paper When Possible

The use of smaller sized billing paper, particularly 5½-by-7-inch sheets, is another simple technique for increasing the client's visual acceptance of a statement. A sheet that is covered with the description of the legal work product impresses the client more than one that has a few lines of text floating in a sea of white. In the latter style, the lawyer's effort appears small and insignificant in the vast expanse of clean paper.

To find out if you can successfully employ this technique, carefully analyze the size of your median bill. Our research in Texas indicates that the median bill in the normal Texas office is about $750. This means that one-half of the bills that we draft will be for less than $750. The letterhead-size billing paper required for the sample bills in Figure 3.1 to 3.4 is obviously inappropriate for detailing a $750 work product. The *effort* detailed is a proportionately small part of the total size of the *physical* bill. The small amount of printing in relation to the large amount of paper visually implies a small amount of work done rather than emphasizing the large amount of *effort* expended. The client's reaction is to suppose that the lawyer hasn't done much work—that is, hasn't expended much *effort*. But when the same amount of typing appears on a small piece of paper, the same client's reaction is quite different. The client now thinks: "How did my lawyer do so much work for such a modest fee?"

**FIGURE 3.3**     **Bill Using Blocking and Punctuation to Project Effort**

Law Offices of Barger & Johnson
1220 E. Dearborn
Suite 2400
Landtown, Wyoming 82111
Ph. 307-747-0033    FAX 307-747-0034
July 28, 1992
Billed through 07/25/92
Bill number 22063-075 DKJ

Landtown Ind. School Dist.
256 Hanover Road
Landtown, Wyoming 82115

General Matters

| | |
|---|---:|
| Balance forward as of bill number 074 dated 07/01/92 | $365.87 |
| Payments received since last bill (last payment 08/17/92) | $365.87 |
| Net balance forward | $.00 |

FOR PROFESSIONAL SERVICES RENDERED

06/29/92—Conferred with Doug Jones about law of individual districts and letter; 06/30/92—Worked on school election problem; Located Eric Bride's paper in *Texas Univ. Seminal* 1991; Briefed the law; 07/01/92—Compared Ashland case; Cursory examination of two basic trials in Ashland case; Determined full text must be secured and examined; 07/01/92—Determined leading cases that control single-member district lawsuits; 07/04/92—Worked on school board brief in single-member question; 07/16/92—Conference with Jones concerning opinion letter; Will be present at school board meeting Monday night at 7:30; 07/19/92—Drafted opinion letter on single-member districts with attachments; 07/20/92—Attended school board meeting and made opinion presentation.

$1,490.00

DISBURSEMENTS
   Copying                                                            112.80

$112.80

BILLING SUMMARY

   TOTAL FEES                                                      $1,602.80

**FIGURE 3.4**     **Bill Using Frequent Action Verbs**

Law Offices of Kelvin, Wyatt and Gray
Two Thompson Center
Suite 1900
Seattle, Washington 98002
Ph. 206-632-5500   FAX 206-632-5502
August 27, 1992
Billed Through 08/23/92
Bill number 21964-008 KLW

Cary Hanks
2700 Bluebell N.W.
Southville, Washington 98333

Divorce/Evelyn Hanks

Balance forward as of bill number 007 dated 07/28/92                    $2,227.52

FOR PROFESSIONAL SERVICES RENDERED

07/23/92—Court appearance; Mason Clinic selected; Met with client after court;
07/27/92—Reviewed entire file; 07/28/92—Telephoned clinic - no test for children; Drafted Order; 07/28/92—Reviewed depo of Mrs. Hanks; 07/30/92—Telephoned Dr. Saniie; Drafted order with rev. req. Dr. Saniie; Telephoned Mr. Ash re: same; 07/31/92—Prepared Order re: psychological examination; 07/31/92—Prepared cover letter to Mr. Ash; 07/31/92—Prepared Protection letter to Hanks; 07/31/92—Made copy of Deposition; 07/31/92—Conferred with Hanks and with Greta Grant; Determined to work on psychological tests and not file interrogatories at this time; 08/04/92—Prepared cover letter to Dr. Saniie; Telephoned Dr. Saniie to get fax number; 08/04/92—Revised letter to client; Mr. Ash; Order re: psychological examination; 08/04/92—Prepared letter to client; 08/05/92—Telephoned Cary Hanks, left message; 08/06/92—Revised letter; Order regarding psychological examination; Sent to client; 08/07/92—Prepared letter to Richard Ash and Dr. Saniie; Prepared letter to Dr. Saniie; 08/07/92—Prepared tabs for exhibits; 08/07/92—Made copies of both depositions and notes; 08/07/92—Telephoned client re: order, client advised order okay; Drafted letter to Ash and Dr. Saniie; 08/12/92—Telephoned Saniie, left message; 08/14/92—Sent copy to client of bill from Dr. Saniie; Prepared cover letter; 08/18/92—Telephoned Saniie, left message; Telephone from client re: status, advised client to send discovery if marriage over; Telephoned Ash re: status, left message; Drafted letter re: same; 08/19/92—Telephone from Dr. Saniie; 08/19/92—Prepared letter to Judge Banner; Prepared letter to Beacom.

                                                                        $822.00

DISBURSEMENTS

| | |
|---|---|
| Long distance | .73 |
| Certified mail | .52 |
| Long distance | .88 |
| Long distance | .13 |
| Copying | 33.45 |
| Copying | 52.50 |
| Postage | .29 |
| Fax transmittal | 18.00 |

```
Cary Hanks
Bill number 21964-008 KLW                              Page 2

Fax transmittal                                          18.00
Long distance                                              .35
Postage                                                    .29
Long distance                                              .25
Long distance                                              .38
                                                      ─────────
                                                       $125.77
BILLING SUMMARY

  TOTAL FEES                                          $822.00

  TOTAL DISBURSEMENTS                                 $125.77
                                                      ─────────
  TOTAL CHARGES FOR THIS BILL                         $947.00

  NET BALANCE FORWARDED                             $2,227.52
                                                      ─────────
  TOTAL BALANCE NOW DUE                             $3,175.29
```

Successfully projecting *effort* on a statement is partly a visual feat, and each of us should take advantage of all possible visual aids. A two-page bill typed on small paper is bound to be more impressive than a one-page bill in which the piece of paper is only partially filled by text. Think about it—it works.

## PROJECT HONESTY, LEGAL ETHICS, AND COMPETENCE

Clients receive a clear impression of the lawyer's honesty and ethics when each individual payment, advance, and cost incurred in a matter is set out clearly in the bill. Figure 3.5 illustrates a method of doing this.

There is another particularly effective way to demonstrate to the client the lawyer's respect for legal ethics and honesty in the billing process. This is when the lawyer deposits funds that belong to the client into the lawyer's trust account and then clearly shows in the billing process the transfer of those funds from the trust account to the firm account as money is used for the benefit of the client or is earned by the lawyer.

In addition, a clear description of the work accomplished for the client is fundamental to the lawyer's projection of competence. In Figure 3.5, the entry of January 10, 1994, concerning examination of bank statements and explanation of court procedure demonstrates the lawyer's knowledge and competence in this field. Other obvious entries might include "Compared facts in this suit with current law" and "Researched damage determination elements."

**FIGURE 3.5**     **Bill Projecting Values and Competence**
**Bill Printed on 5⅜ by 5½ Inch Stationary**

---

Law Offices of
Martinez & Gonzalez
1720 Oak Street
Lakewood, New Jersey 08701
908-591-0122

April 30, 1994

Judy Walden
328 Greenview Road
Lakewood, New Jersey 08715

For Professional Services

1/02/94—Conferred with client concerning decision to secure a divorce; drafted petition for divorce with Temporary Order prayer; Prepared petition and Temporary Restraining Order; Secured setting date for Temporary Order hearing; Prepared notice to client of date; Secured signature of petitioner on affidavit; Notarized statement; Filed pleadings; Made appointment for client to be prepared for temporary hearing; 1/10/94—Developed financial facts from client's examined bank statements and cost of living materials; Explained court procedure and suggested proper dress; 1/11/94—Tried Temporary Order petition; Recorded judgment facts given by judge from bench with log entry; Prepared temporary order; Mailed copy to client; Secured court's signature on order.

| | |
|---|---:|
| Total fee thus far earned | $431.00 |
| Filing fee for petition with T.R.O. | 125.00 |
| Total amount received | 750.00 |
| Credit Balance | ($194.00) |

---

One word to avoid in work description is *briefed*. Clients, in my experience, are happy to pay for the research of points of law applicable to the particular case and for the comparison of the law of the jurisdiction with the facts in the case. *Briefed* used in a bill suggests to many clients something that the lawyer should have learned in law school. The best bills do not use this word to describe the research process.

## PROJECT FAIRNESS

The client's expectations about the amount of the fee are infinitely more important to the client's acceptance of the fee amount than is the actual amount.

An inadequate fee estimate that results in a bill in excess of the estimate almost always produces a bad effect on the client. Current research shows that if the initial fee estimate proves wrong but is then corrected by the lawyer before it becomes a fact, the ultimate fee will be perceived as fair by the client. The client will not be surprised—and will not feel deceived.

Any manual system will allow for daily time and bookkeeping entries and an accurate determination of when a fee estimate becomes inadequate. However, the easiest procedure is to use good computer software that updates money and time charges daily. Within one to two minutes a lawyer, secretary, or legal assistant can be provided a current bill printout for every file on which the legal team is working.

All files pulled for work need to be accompanied by updated billing information to eliminate the surprise—to both lawyer and client—of wrong estimates that remain uncorrected. It is a simple rule, but one that ensures there is ample time and notice to correct an incorrect fee estimate or fee agreement.

To draft bills that clients rush to pay, lawyers must fully understand how the fee amount estimate impacts the client's perception of the bill's fairness.

## FORMAT THE BILL APPROPRIATELY

The manner in which component value billing is expressed on the fee statement depends on the firm's billing customs and systems.

If the firm's statements normally do not list hours worked but describe the work done for the client, list reimbursable items (such as postage, telephone, fax, and copying charges), and show a fee amount for legal services, no change is needed. The component method of calculation is used by the firm to determine what the legal service is worth, that is, what the fee amount will be. This type of statement format should always be used unless the client requests additional information.

If the statement to the client normally describes the work done for the client, provides hourly information, and lists reimbursable expenses, this component method follows the same pattern. In the section in which hours are multiplied by rates, for example, there is no change in people charges. Rather, the list of people is expanded to include the entire staff that worked in tandem to render the legal service. If you calculate a receptionist's time on a standard charge per contact, the statement merely shows communication contacts with a figure. Finding the right words to express the calculation comes with experience and suggestions from your staff.

Some firms prefer to show charges for document construction (which expresses the per-page equipment component) under reimbursable expenses along with copying costs. My own preference is to list the item "document construction" along with the other parts of the legal service fee and not in the reimbursable expenses column.

Charges to the client for electronic research can be titled as such or perhaps as "electronic doctrine verification." The use of electronic research systems is a lawyering tool and not a reimbursable expense.

The charge should be shown as such a component along with the people charges for the legal service on the expanded bill, if requested.

For the use of systems or software, the charge is listed in the legal service section of the bill. The statement may show "Will library, $25," or perhaps "Document creations, $85."

## DRAFT AN INVITING STATEMENT

When it comes to the projection of effort, there is an analytical way even for drafting bills. I try to refrain from discussing cases that I win, but I'll make an exception so that I can share a particular bill. The following references a true case, but the names, dates, and number of the court have otherwise been changed.

I was employed, in a community with less than 30,000 people, to represent a doctor whose wife had sued him for divorce. The doctor used an accounting firm in the Dallas area that referred him to a Dallas law firm that then engaged me to prepare the lawsuit for trial in Greenville, Texas.

> May 24, 1994, conference with CPA Sam Hapgood, in preparation for deposition; May 25, 1994, taking of deposition of Mrs. Smith and appearance at deposition of Dr. Smith; May 28, 1994, conference with Guy Billout concerning child support, alimony, and visitation rights; June 17, 1994, secured case setting for June 23, 1994; June 18, 1994, conference by phone with Dr. Smith concerning alimony and child support possibilities; June 19, 1994, conference concerning amendments to pleadings; June 22, 1994, conference by phone with cocounsel concerning briefing on parental rights and conference by phone with Dr. Smith concerning appearance at trial; June 23, 1994, construction of trial briefs for presentation to Judge Rolwing, establishing that adoptive husband has same position as blood husband in the State of Texas and trial of the motion to show cause in the 162 Judicial District Court; June 29, 1994, conference by phone with cocounsel concerning possibility of early trial to relieve high alimony figure, something over $850 per month, the highest ever awarded in the County of Naught; July 4, 1994, study of proposed settlement arrangement; July 8, 1994, conference with cocounsel concerning counteroffer proposition; July 15, 1994, examination of proposition of money sources; August 17, 1994, examination of settlement, proposal of a receivership, and a possible complete destruction of the estate of Dr. and Mrs. Smith; August 20, 1994, discussion with cocounsel concerning involvement of Attorney Brown and his recommendation of a possible money-lender; August 21, 1994, conference with Dr. Smith concerning money source, Brown offer, relative values under Medicare, hospital, and farm property, and determination to seek receivership and public sale of properties; August 25, 1994, conference with cocounsel to confirm rejections of both offers; September 2, 1994, conference with Johnson and Jones to finalize arrangements for trial dates and real estate appraisals by experts; September 8, 1994, conference with John Jones concerning standards that must be applied and appraisal for use of testimony in court; September 11, 1994, appeared at the call of the docket of the 18th Judicial District Court and secured a setting for October 4, 1994, for trial; September 15, 1994, conference with cocounsel by phone concerning

depreciation of value of hospital properties based on the adoption of Medicare program under Social Security; August 24, 1994, conference with Johnson, Jones, and Dr. Smith concerning values; September 28, 1994, conference concerning settlement figures; September 30, 1994, conference with cocounsel concerning final settlement approved by Dr. Smith; October 4, 1994, appearance at the call of the week's docket to secure postponement of the suit, on the ground of settlement in process, until October 8, 1994; October 8, 1994, secured a settlement continuance until jury week of October 11; October 13, 1994, secured definite setting with Judge Elonzo for 2:30, October 18, 1994, for trial and proof of property arrangement; October 18, 1994, proof in court of property settlement and permitted proof and divorce ground, approval of judgment, drafting of judgment, and entry of the judgment.

Aren't you tired from reading this bill? You can feel the effort that went into this matter, real effort. Everything here is true and the client knew it—and paid me the day he got the bill. It takes pages and pages without paragraphs to show the effort, but when it is done, the fee figure in the bill is unimportant in comparison to the effort, which stands out all over.

I highly recommend that you divide the work out, listing the date the work is done, but never the number of hours that were involved. This is your information for billing purposes: an adequate description of what you have done, never just *briefing*. This is how effort is projected in the actual bill.

### Personalize the Bill

After the final fee amount is stated, you will find a warmer reception for your fee by adding a personal comment that permits the reader to feel that your effort (and the effort of your firm) was expended for something more altruistic than mere money. For example, following a Section 1244 Corporation Organization, a statement like this is appropriate and warmly received: "We hope this corporate venture will be as successful as all the facts we now have indicate. We appreciate your confidence and your practice tremendously." Or, at the end of an adoption bill, words like these may be used to great advantage: "We appreciate your confidence and patience very much. I know you are going to enjoy enormously having John Marshall Smith in your home." A handwritten note can also be very effective.

Never forget that you do not bill a corporation. Every corporation has an employee who is a human being and who reads and evaluates your bill. A bill to a corporation can be ended with words like these: "We greatly appreciate this opportunity of service to your organization. See Figures 3.6 to 3.8 for samples of personalized bills.

### Timing the Bill

If you offer a bill within a month of the work's completion, you will collect more than 95 percent of the total amount. This figure is very conservative. You will normally collect 100 percent. If you wait longer than three months, you really should be embarrassed to send a bill at all. You must bill promptly—and have a system for doing so.

### Include the Basis for Reimbursable Expenses

Another suggestion is that all reimbursable expenses be set out following the fee figure. In each instance, the date on which the reimbursement expense was incurred should be stated. If mileage is involved, the exact basis on which the charges are made should be clearly explained.

## MAKE THE BILL COMPLETE

Here is one last warning: Make every bill complete. Be sure to list everything you have done for the client—every bit of effort you've expended. The client is entitled to each detail.

And here is one last suggestion: Never decide on the final amount of the bill until you have finished reviewing it. You may find that you

**FIGURE 3.6**       **Personalized Bill: Sample I**

Law Offices of
FLEMING Q. SCHLOSSER
2719 N. Jefferson
Suite 3200
Chattanooga, Tennessee 37422
728-5306
Area Code 615

February 27, 1994

Mr. E.E. Wilson
527 Soup Creek
Chattanooga, Tennessee 37466

STATEMENT

January 2, 1994, Conference to determine need for contract to establish in provable form the relationship of an independent contractor; February 16, 1994, Drafting of proposed contract upon the briefing of elements of an independent contractor's characteristics; February 24, 1994, Delivery of contract with approval of form. Total, $75.00. February 24, 1994, Duplication expense of forms in published form for use, $15.60. Gross Total, $90.60.

I appreciate enormously your confidence and your practice. This plan should allow you to handle each job on individual basis with maximum safety from liability.

**FIGURE 3.7**          **Personalized Bill: Sample 2**

---

F Q S

Statement

Law Offices of
FELICIA A. SCHLOSSER
2719 N. Jefferson
Suite 3200
Chattanooga, Tennessee 37422
728-5306
Area Code 615

February 27, 1994

Mr. E.E. Wilson
527 Soup Creek
Chattanooga, Tennessee 37466

---

For Professional Services

January 2, 1994, Conference to determine need for contract to establish in provable form the relationship of an independent contractor; February 16, 1994, Drafting of proposed contract upon the briefing of elements of an independent contractor's characteristics; February 24, 1994, Delivery of contract with approval of form. Total, $75.00. February 24, 1994, Duplication expense of forms in published form for use, $15.60.

GROSS TOTAL . . . . . . $90.60

I appreciate enormously your confidence and your practice. This plan should allow you to handle each job on individual basis with maximum safety from liability.

---

have a little client in you too. When you finish your review, you too may wonder how you performed such excellent service in such a businesslike manner, projected in proper form to a client, for such a modest fee. Let your conscience, your time records, your responsibility, and your values toward the client be your guide.

**FIGURE 3.8**     **Personalized Bill: Sample 3**

Law Offices of
LAFEVER, ABRIL & CUSIC
117 W. Thorn Street
15th Floor
St. Paul, Minnesota 55160
438-1124
Area Code 612

May 1, 1994

Mr. Howard Risatti
5113 Fieldbrook Drive
Sandton, Minnesota 54222

STATEMENT

| | |
|---|---|
| March 17, 1994 | Drafted letter of notice to C.A. Kline with copy to Bob Franklin of damage claim. |
| April 3, 1994 | Conference with insurance adjuster with determination that settlement has been offered but no tender can be made until easements may be drawn. Determination that no easements may be drawn until City Engineer determines work plan and approves drainage system for underground pipe. |
| April 21, 1994 | Conference in City Hall with Snyder to determine when City may produce easement location description. |
| April 29, 1994 | Drafted two requisite easements under description provided by City. Conference with Bob Franklin to determine manner of execution. Delivery of easements to Franklin. |
| May 13, 1994 | Conference with C.A. Kline with explanation that no easement may be drafted until City acts and City cannot act until engineer is employed. |
| July 29, 1994 | Delivery of petition to Long Insurance Agency. Conference with City Manager to determine when we can expect City Engineering Department to function. |

Total . . . . . . . . . . . . . . . . . . . . . . . . . . . . . . . . . . . . . . . . . . . . . . . . . . . . . . . . . . . . . . . . . . . . . . . . . .$150.00

I appreciate your practice and confidence and am glad this matter seems to be terminated once and for all.  E.L. Cusic

# CHAPTER **IV**

# Employing Other Techniques that Project Effort

Along with the billing methods discussed throughout this book, several other techniques can be effectively employed to project your effort on the client's behalf. When used correctly, these techniques work in concert with your billing methods to effect total client satisfaction. These techniques include:

● Copying the client on key matters
● Giving the client undivided attention during meetings
● Keeping good work records
● Using a proper timekeeping system.

## COPY THE CLIENT ON ALL KEY MATTERS

Copying the client on all key matters requires only 15 to 30 minutes per day, and it makes a great difference in the effort you project to your client. Every piece of key correspondence arriving in the office should immediately be photocopied, "For Your Information" and mailed to the client, without a letter of enclosure. The same procedure should be used for every written work product, every letter that is written, every offer that is made, and every trial brief that is developed for the client's case or matter.

Clients should be given their own document file so that they are aware of all the work that you complete on their behalf as it is completed. However, be clear on whether the client needs to respond or take any action on the items sent. Stamp "No Response Required" or "Response Requested" to make it clear when client action is needed.

Every deposition taken has a client copy. Those of us who have worked on the plaintiff's side of the docket know that perhaps the most difficult job of the plaintiff's lawyer is to teach the client to tell the truth prior to the deposition. How difficult it is to take a person unskilled in the English language and teach that person how to tell the truth, in English, so that it sounds, reads, and is the truth. You will find that when you provide clients with a copy of their own deposition, they are constantly reminded of the effort that you have expended on their behalf.

There is a side benefit to copying clients on critical documentation, particularly depositions. Clients do not put their depositions in the study or even in the living room. They put them on the cocktail table in the den and they read them to their neighbors, their cousins, and their preachers. As a result, there are very few questions that an insurance lawyer can ever ask them for which they don't remember their response.

## GIVE THE CLIENT UNDIVIDED ATTENTION IN ALL MEETINGS

When people come into our offices, what are they asking for? Results? Oh, they'd like to have results, and our pride will get the results; we are result-oriented. What clients want most is effort-orientation. We can show effort by giving them our undivided attention.

This means, of course, that we must turn off the telephone. If we are to project effort, we must give our undivided attention to the client in the minutes that the client is in our presence. I don't mean to indicate that critical people can't reach me by telephone, or that the President would not be most welcome. However, he has not had occasion to call me recently, and I suspect he hasn't called you, either. Except in the most pressing circumstances, phone calls can be returned.

## KEEP GOOD RECORDS OF COMPLETED WORK

Lawyers who want to master the billing techniques described in these pages need to build the discipline of keeping detailed logs in their time sheets, describing what work was completed and all contacts made, by name and nature of the contact. As a result, the bill will read like a story, not a telegram. It will have a plot, with a beginning, middle, and end, and will use the real names of the characters involved.

## USE A TIMEKEEPING SYSTEM

We have heard for years that timekeepers make 40 percent more money than nontimekeepers. The 33 percent or so of lawyers who always keep time records are the ones with the discipline. Ask yourself the question, How many hours do you earn and do you charge? Lawyers who are timekeepers can always tell you, and clients can rely on what they say.

If you are to survive economically, you must be an "always timekeeper." So set an hourly rate based on *something*. Most clients are just as willing to pay you $200 as they are $100, if you just go about collecting it in the right way.

There are many systems that will allow you to do a good time-keeping job. But you have to have a system to develop the always-timekeeping habit; and the habit has to protect you. The system that I describe below is a system—yet it is not the only system. In my judgment, it works best for lawyer's who are solos or practice in a small group of two to four lawyers. If there are more than four lawyers in your firm, I would recommend another system. There are many to choose from. For a good reference, see Resources for Choosing Time and Billing Software on page 59.

**Timekeeping In Action**

When Mr. Jones comes into your office in the morning, you reach into the desk, lift up a time sheet, write his name on the time sheet (putting it so Mr. Jones can see it), and record the time. Mr. Jones wants to talk to you because he is selling a portion of a lot that he owns down the street from his house. He wants to know if you will represent him in the matter and if you will see about drafting the deed and the need for an abstract of title insurance. Then you discuss the consideration, which is $15,000, and how it is to be paid, and you write down all the things involved. It takes three-tenths of an hour. You mark the time the discussion is concluded in front of Mr. Jones. He sees you put three-tenths of an hour on the sheet and circle it. You pull it apart and put the white copy in his file if he has one. If not, you put the copy in a file basket. You drop the yellow copy behind the *J* for Jones and give the pink copy to him. Then you talk about the problems of the United Presbyterian Church, where you are both elders, and he knows that the discussion of the church is not being charged to his account—but he knows that the discussion at your desk will be on the statement.

Mr. Jones leaves, the telephone rings, you answer it, and pick up a time slip. The caller says, "This is Mrs. Smith, I wonder if you have heard anything about the divorce." You put the name down and the time she calls, give her the information, and charge her for two-tenths of an hour—and you mark it down. You pull the sheet apart, and the white copy goes in Mrs. Smith's file, the yellow one goes behind Mrs. Smith's name, and the pink one is saved for the client.

Now you need to go back and see what you are going to tell the judge in a few minutes when you're in court on a motion to show cause whether the 10-day rule really has an exception. You are to do this for a man named Morgan. You write down the date and time, do the necessary briefing, and basically record what you have done. You check the motion to show cause and the citation is no good because it hasn't been filed for the 10 days. You pull the time sheet apart; place the white one in the client's file, the yellow one behind the client's name, and save the pink one for the client.

A client calls as you're walking out the door. After the client's call is finished, you take that time slip and put it in your coat that very moment. When you come back to the office, by absolute rote memory, you pull it out and put the three copies in the appropriate places.

## Develop The Habit

In the first month of becoming a full-time timekeeper, one goes through an experience that is as bad as stopping smoking. The second month is just as bad as the second month of not smoking. In the third month, for about 25 percent of the time one does continual timekeeping without the horror of feeling like Pavlov's dog. After six months, timekeeping becomes almost a habit that you can rely on, so that when the telephone rings, you reach for the time slip and begin to write. After a year, you develop paresis of the brain. You cannot talk to a judge or to a client or to anyone without having recorded the client's name on a time slip and had the joy of pulling it apart. It cannot be done by sometimes-timekeepers. It can only be done by always-timekeepers.

So what happens to those sheets once you have them in the file? Every once in a while I am fortunate enough to have a client who says, "Harris, what do I owe you?" I do nothing to discourage this marvelous question, and never let it be said that I can't answer the client. I look at the file and can immediately say, "Well, let's see, John, you were here last Thursday and we had a conference about the sale, and we drafted the instruments for you Saturday morning, and we closed Tuesday." I add up what I have on time and find that it's one-eight of an hour, so I say, "John, you owe me $145," and he writes out a check. I place the time slips on the outside of the file, and the slips are marked "paid." My secretary takes these time slips and pulls the duplicates out of the billing box and drops them into the file marked "paid." This way nothing is in the billing box that's been paid.

There are clients who would never ask what they owed even if we waited until the end of the millennium. They have to be reminded frequently, and you must have a system to handle this. On the 28th of every month, a secretary in my office alphabetizes the billing box, based on the client's name and file number. If you have four Jones matters, each Jones matter is separated by paper clips. I personally look at all the *A*'s, and I bill everybody in *A* that I feel I reasonably can. I bill these cases every month, whether the case is finished or not. I dictate the bill, and the secretary types it in an original and one copy. Attached to the copy is the yellow billing slip. The original has nothing attached to it, and it is sent to the client. When the client sends the check, the secretary marks the copy bill with "paid" and the date it is paid. That copy, with the time slips on the back, is dropped into the client's file.

Nothing that has been billed ever remains alphabetized in the billing box, and nothing that has ever been paid ever remains in the back of the billing box. At any moment we can tell, by a very simple system and without any secretarial help at all, how many hours of chargeable time we have in our accounts receivable that we have not billed, and how much billing we have done for which we have not collected. That is virtually all the control that one needs in the billing.

Every Friday before I leave the office, I go through the billing file to see the hours charged as of that date. This allows me to know, week by week, month by month, and year by year, exactly what my chargeable time is—compared to the clock hours I spend at the office.

Lawyers in small firms or practicing alone are able to bill slightly more than half of the time that they are at the office. If you keep records, you will find that this is exactly right. If you work an eight-hour day, your chance of billing beyond four or so hours is very slight. If you are in a large firm, one of the reasons the firm can and does make more money than most solo practitioners is that the firm has an organization that protects you in the office. It is true that partners in large firms do bill more than 2,000 hours a year—some of them bill as many as 2,500 hours. But it is a rare thing for solo practitioners or those in firms of less than four lawyers to do this.

Again, keep in mind that the client's chief concern is not about the fee. If you can understand that, the rest will fall into place. Clients want you to take good care of them. Service is the thing, not time billing. The bill should capture the value delivered and tell the story of the case.

# CHAPTER V

# Putting the Commandments on Drafting Bills into Action

Drafting bills clients will rush to pay is a skill that can be learned. The basic plan is to study the guidelines that clients have given us in the two major client analyses of our profession: the Prentice-Hall Missouri Motivational Study of 1960 and Barbara Curran's American Bar Foundation study, "The Legal Needs of the Public". From these we can establish criteria for creating a bill the client will rush to pay. Bills for legal services must meet five clear goals, which lawyers should perceive as commandments.

1. The bill must project effort.
2. The bill must demonstrate concern for the client and the client's case.
3. The bill must evidence a high standard of honesty and legal ethics.
4. The bill must reveal the lawyer's basic competence in the field.
5. The bill amount must be perceived by the client as a "fair fee."

## A SUMMARY OF HIGHLY EFFECTIVE TECHNIQUES

To project effort and concern, every bill must describe all actions taken on behalf of the client by the *entire* legal services delivery team. If only the lawyer's effort is delineated, the bill usually fails to fully describe the service rendered. The work description should not delineate what service was rendered by what staff member, however.

To give the right impact to each description of work done, verbs and verb-related words should be used. Verbs project effort, movement, and active concern. Nouns describe a condition or thing that the client must translate into an action or concern. The words *will* and *trust* do not have the impact of *drafted will* or *drafted trust* in the context of a bill for legal services. Well-drafted bills are laced with action verbs like these: filed, mailed, copied, outlined, deposed, contacted, secured, determined, concluded, improved, rejected, proposed, suggested, calculated, examined, compared, searched, researched, briefed, drafted, prepared, constructed, closed, engaged, demanded, complied, revised, updated, redacted.

Seldom refer to a telephone call as simply a telephone call. A phone call is, in fact, a conference and deserves the dignity of a conference in billing. Accordingly, the word *conference* should always be accompanied by a verb phrase detailing the item discussed. For example, the description "Conference with defendant's lawyer to discuss temporary child support amount and to determine the date on which the defendant will begin making payments" projects effort. Compare this with "Conference with defendant's lawyer" or, even worse, simply "Conference."

With experience, certain verbs will be reserved for specific staff functions. For example, lawyers *draft* a document, and word processors and secretaries *prepare* a document in the billing process.

Here's another tip for effectively describing the legal services delivered. There is a temptation to use abbreviations in billing information—particularly with older software packages that limit the length of descriptions on bills printed by the computer system. Such abbreviations as C/W, TF, and TT for "Conferred with," "Telephone from," or "Telephone to" may be recognized by some clients but not by all, and so should be resisted. Abbreviations don't project effort and concern to many readers of our bills. A better plan for computer billing systems with limitations on the number of words per entry is to adopt the multiple entry per day method shown in Figure 3.5.

In addition to a verb-rich description of work done (with a date assigned to each entry), a block billing form is recommended for statements. Use of the block form without paragraphs, dividing work products with semicolons only (not periods), permits the eye and mind to move smoothly from work product to work product. The sample statement in Figure 3.3 illustrates the impact of a block bill prepared without a computer program.

Some computer programs require that the date of services always be flush with the left margin. Such programs can be used to produce effective bills if the bills are formatted in the modified block form with no lines left blank between descriptive work entries. For the bill to project effort most effectively, the continuous nature of the lawyer's effort and concern must be visually demonstrated, as in the modified block form bill in Figure 3.8.

A bill that correctly lists all work products after the date completed but then leaves blank lines before the next date on which services are listed visually reduces the impact of the work done. Instead of giving the desired perception that many different work products were provided (as accomplished by the bill in Figure 3.8), the impact of such a bill is that only a few services were rendered.

For bills that clients rush to pay, whether prepared with a typewriter, word processor, or time and billing system, the size of the billing paper should be adjusted to permit the work product description and financial information to dominate the space. A bill with few words or figures and much blank white space does not provide the visual projection of effort and concern that is given by a bill with extensive written material and little white space. A bill with nine lines of text should not be presented on full-size stationery, leaving 64 lines of blank space. A small five-by-eight inch sheet of billing paper is preferable.

No revelation of the number of hours expended should be made in the standard bill. Some lawyers make exceptions for insurance company clients, but the better practice is to recognize that the hours expended are part of the cost accounting analysis and that time alone is not a proper evaluation of the skill, responsibility, and worth of a lawyer's service. Your minimum charge for a service should ideally be based on three factors: 1) the time expended, 2) the value of the service to the client, and 3) the responsibility borne by the lawyer. A bill emphasizing hours only is projecting only one-third of the effort and risk factors involved.

As a final touch, nothing shows client concern more clearly than a handwritten note immediately after the words "Please pay this amount," following the final entry. In a residential real estate closing, for example, you might write: "Thank you for permitting me to represent you in this closing on your home. I know you will enjoy the neighborhood. JQA." In an adoption the note might read: "I know you will enjoy having John Smith Jones II in your home and in your life. JQA." A corporate client should never be billed without a written thank you for the business which might read like this: "We appreciate your business and your confidence in us very much. JQA."

## WHY CLIENTS RETURN TO YOU

The Missouri Motivational Study divided participants into two groups based on their response to the question, "Would you employ the lawyer that you employed in the last event again?" Those who replied in the affirmative were put in one group, and those who replied in the negative were put in another. Each was then asked the reason for their response. This is the most revealing section in the Missouri Motivational Study.

You may expect a common response to be "I like my lawyer and I would certainly employ her again because she won my case." You find it. It's not there. You might look for "Because he certainly was reasonable in his charges." Find it. It's not there.

What answers are there? "I would employ her again because of her friendliness." "I like the way he came out in the waiting room and took my hand and said, 'John, I'm so glad to see you. Won't you please come in?'" "I like the prompt businesslike manner." "I like the ways she talked about what the fee was going to be, as if it had some importance to both of us, at the very beginning of the employment." "I like the way he billed me every month for reimbursements that he had." These comments also appeared in the Missouri Motivational

Study responses. "I like the way she itemized the bill so I knew what I was paying for." "I loved his courtesy, the way he kept the telephone turned off when I was discussing a matter with him and how he would protect my confidences." "I like the way he was not condescending." "She even sent me trial briefs and let me know that I could understand some of these instruments just as well as she could, and she discussed the case fully, and kept me informed. I knew exactly what was going on all the time." Now, I call your attention to the facts. The people who pay you and me wrote these comments. These are the things clients like in lawyers that get the repeat business.

You may anticipate replies of "I wouldn't hire him if he was the last lawyer in Missouri. He lost my case." Find it. It's not there. Or "She overcharged me" or "He's too expensive." Find it. It's not there.

Responses to the query "Why wouldn't you hire the lawyer again?" ran like this. "Well, I certainly couldn't stand his impersonal attitude. He was so busy that I was just a file number and he didn't even know my name or who I was. When I would ask if he had heard anything, he would look at me like he wondered who I was and what he should have heard." "She was so bored and indifferent." "He always had so many papers on his desk he didn't have time to fool with my $1 million case. He was certainly rude and brusque. He didn't have time to get up and usher me out and usher me in. He listened to everybody on the telephone and talked about people's business on the telephone, which horrified me." "She had a superior attitude and never told me anything because, of course, I am too stupid. I was a layperson and she was a smart lawyer. I don't know the English language. I couldn't understand about rules of law. I was a stupid idiot. I wouldn't hire her again because she had a superior arrogant attitude and failed to keep me informed. I never knew what was going on." "He never tells us whether he won or lost."

As these comments show, you lose clients by not understanding what clients want. Clients want a businesslike approach and it is incumbent upon you and me to see that they get it. This is the true test for lawyers. It is not the fee setting or fee amount that turns clients against lawyers—it is the way we handle our individual business.

# Postscript: Timekeeping and Billing Tips

by Fran Shellenberger

To bill successfully, lawyers must become master timekeepers. There's only one way to keep time—*contemporaneously* as the work is being done. Every method of keeping time—paper slips, cards, sheets, voice dictation, or direct entry by the lawyer into a computer—will actually lose time if it is not captured contemporaneously.

The problem with most law firm billing systems is that time is entered into the computer at the time when the firm should instead be reviewing draft bills and work-in-progress reports. Lawyers fail to write up their time until a day or two before bills should be mailed. When delays are tolerated, Harris Morgan's suggestions regarding projection of effort and the client's appreciation are sabotaged with unfortunate results:

- Lawyers underbill clients because they don't know how much to charge and they must avoid overcharging.
- Lawyers overbill clients for the same reasons, but the projection of effort is lost because much of it is forgotten. They know clients are quick to object and lawyers are helpless against these complaints when accurate time records aren't there to back up the bill.
- Bills are delayed. Review and editing of bills cannot occur until time is entered; therefore, Morgan's suggestions for timing the arrival of bills according to the client's appreciation curve are lost.
- Clients are slower to pay a lawyer's bill when it is delayed.

## TIPS ON BEING A MASTER TIMEKEEPER

Use software, such as *Timeslips,* that "pops up" on your computer network so you can enter the time as a byproduct of your work. The time goes directly into the program and the computer watches the clock. You can generate a bill this afternoon for work completed this morning.

If your computer is not on a network or you don't have access to network software, use a separate program such as *PCTime* to capture the time. From *PCTime*, data can be entered into the firm's billing program via a floppy disk.

If you write timeslips or sheets, keep a supply of them in your briefcase, at home, and in your car, so you can keep time contemporaneously wherever you're working. If you wait until you get to the office to capture the time, you'll forget important details (so you can't completely project effort).

If you dictate time, use a separate unit (the hand-held type) so your time entry is not delayed until your correspondence and documents are transcribed. A separate unit allows support staff to transcribe and enter the time every day. Keep a dictation unit at home, in your car, and in your briefcase too. Otherwise you'll lose or delay time.

Whatever your method for capturing time, write it or dictate it just as you want the client to see it, as though you are explaining to the client the work being done. This is important to

● Project effort, as Morgan recommends
● Minimize or eliminate editing and rewriting of bills
● Save lawyer time during the review process
● Minimize editing pre-bills into final bills at the computer (a major cause of delays).
● Speed up mailing of the final bill

Choose software that allows generous narrative for describing services. Early versions of time and billing software often limited the number of characters for describing services, focusing on the *time* rather than the *effort*. These bills fostered complaints about hourly billing—a problem that the legal industry has not yet overcome.

Lawyers will encounter resistance from administrative staff who want brief narratives to expedite time entry. Staff need to be educated regarding the wish for clients to rush to pay bills and the need for projecting effort and concern, as Morgan recommends. All those verbs are what generate the income to pay staff salaries. The goal is to be *effective* in client billing, even at the expense of perceived *efficiency* of limited narrative.

It is crucial to capture *all* your time even if you're not sure it's billable. If necessary, you can make the decision to write off time when reviewing preliminary bills. One method of handling nonbillable time is to include the item (projecting effort) on the bill and to note that there is no charge in the hours column on the final bill. It's good client relations to let the client know that you do not bill for everything, that some services have been provided (that is, effort has been expended) at no charge. If you place a telephone call and leave a message with a secretary, show that on the bill at no charge. This tells the client you've been attentive and made an effort on the client's behalf.

## TIPS ON BETTER BILLING

There are often loose time and expense charges that occur after a matter is resolved, usually within three to six months. Inform clients you will send a cleanup bill for these items several months hence. That way the client expects another small bill, and you won't have to absorb that time and expense.

If a bill is not paid within 30 days, begin the collection process promptly. This method has proven highly effective. If you do not make an effort to collect after 30 days, you are giving the client permission not to pay for another 30 or 60 days.

Morgan suggests that if your billing system is on a network, you can offer to check the status (accrued time, etc.) of the client's account while the client is in your office. If you're not on a network, you can request a printout while the client is present. In both instances, the client is impressed with your businesslike approach to billing and fully comprehends the time (effort) and fee amount already incurred. In some instances, the client will write a check on the spot.

No client will rush to pay a bill that comes as a surprise, or worse, a shock. Relay any bad news regarding the bill in person or by telephone before putting it in the mail.

## CONCLUSION

There are many other technques for improving your timekeeping and billing practices. Once you decide to employ Morgan's philosophy, you will find yourself discovering new approaches that improve results. In the final analysis, J. Harris Morgan has provided a blueprint for you to follow—a plan that will allow you to draft bills that clients rush to pay.

# About the Authors

**J. Harris Morgan** is a partner of Morgan & Gotcher in Greenville, Texas, specializing in elder care, domestic relations, probate, estate planning, and business law. A recognized expert in time and billing systems and renowned for his approach to drafting bills, Harris is a prolific author and speaker on billing and quality-service issues. He is a former Chair of the Section of Law Practice Management, a member of the Section's Honorary Council, an American Bar Foundation Fellow, and Chair of the Supreme Court of Texas's Task Force on Improving the Efficiency of the Court System in Texas.

**Julie M. Tamminen** practiced employment law in Minnesota before moving to New York and changing to the field of Human Resources Management. She has worked for Fortune 100 Corporations, specializing in equal employment opportunity and human relations, and has authored several publications on law firm management. She is the author of the recently released book *Sexual Harassment in the Workplace: Managing Corporate Policy* and writes a regular column in the New York State Bar News entitled "Communicating with Your Client," focusing on how lawyers can improve client relations. She is a member of the LPM Publishing Board and is currently working on a book about stress management for lawyers.

**Fran Shellenberger** is with Ogletree Deakins Nash Smoak & Stewart, a 100-attorney firm in Washington, D.C. specializing in labor employment and environmental matters. She has previously run her own consulting firm and worked in five law firms in four states. At the invitation of the ABA, she became one of the first Associate members in 1983. She currently serves as the Computer and Technology Division Liaison to Membership for the Section of Law Practice Management.

# APPENDIX A

# ABA Model Rule 1.5 of Professional Conduct

## RULE 1.5 FEES

(a) A lawyer's fee shall be reasonable. The factors to be considered in determining the reasonableness of a fee include the following:

(1) the time and labor required, the novelty and difficulty of the questions involved, and the skill requisite to perform the legal service properly;

(2) the likelihood, if apparent to the client, that the acceptance of the particular employment will preclude other employment by the lawyer;

(3) the fee customarily charged in the locality for similar legal services;

(4) the amount involved and the results obtained;

(5) the time limitations imposed by the client or by the circumstances;

(6) the nature and length of the professional relationship with the client;

(7) the experience, reputation, and ability of the lawyer or lawyers performing the services; and

(8) whether the fee is fixed or contingent.

(b) When the lawyer has not regularly represented the client, the basis or rate of the fee shall be communicated to the client, preferably in writing, before or within a reasonable time after commencing the representation.

(c) A fee may be contingent on the outcome of the matter for which the service is rendered, except in a matter in which a contingent fee is prohibited by paragraph (d) or other law. A contingent fee agreement shall be in writing and shall state the method by which the fee is to be determined, including the percentage or percentages that shall accrue to the lawyer in the event of settlement, trial or appeal, litigation and other expenses to be deducted from the recovery, and whether such expenses are to be deducted before or after the contingent fee is calculated. Upon conclusion of a contingent fee matter, the lawyer shall provide the client with a written statement stating the outcome of the matter and, if there is a recovery, showing the remittance to the client and the method of its determination.

(d) A lawyer shall not enter into an arrangement for, charge, or collect:

(1) any fee in a domestic relations matter, the payment or amount of which is contingent upon the securing of a divorce or upon the amount of alimony or support, or property settlement in lieu thereof; or

(2) a contingent fee for representing a defendant in a criminal case.

(e) A division of a fee between lawyers who are not in the same firm may be made only if:

(1) the division is in proportion to the services performed by each lawyer or, by written agreement with the client, each lawyer assumes joint responsibility for the representation;

(2) the client is advised of and does not object to the participation of all the lawyers involved; and

(3) the total fee is reasonable.

## COMMENT

### Basis of Rate of Fee

When the lawyer has regularly represented a client, they ordinarily will have evolved an understanding concerning the basis or rate of the fee. In a new client-lawyer relationship, however, an understanding as to the fee should be promptly established. It is not necessary to recite all the factors that underlie the basis of the fee, but only those that are directly involved in its computation. It is sufficient, for example, to state that the basic rate is an hourly charge or a fixed amount or an estimated amount, or to identify the factors that may be taken into account in finally fixing the fee. When developments occur during the representation that render an earlier estimate substantially inaccurate, a revised estimate should be provided to the client. A written statement concerning the fee reduces the possibility of misunderstanding. Furnishing the client with a simple memorandum or a copy of the lawyer's customary fee schedule is sufficient if the basis or rate of the fee is set forth.

### Terms of Payment

A lawyer may require advance payment of a fee, but is obliged to return any unearned portion. See Rule 1.16(d). A lawyer may accept property in payment for services, such as an ownership interest in an enterprise, providing this does not involve acquisition of a proprietary interest in the cause of action or subject matter of the litigation contrary to Rule 1.8(j). However, a fee paid in property instead of money may be subject to special scrutiny because it involves questions concerning special value of the services and the lawyer's special knowledge of the value of the property.

An agreement may not be made whose terms might induce the lawyer improperly to curtail services for the client or perform them in a way contrary to the client's interest. For example, a lawyer should not enter into an agreement whereby services are to be provided only up to a stated amount when it is foreseeable that more extensive services probably will be required, unless the situation is adequately explained to the client. Otherwise, the client might have to bargain for further assistance in the midst of a proceeding or transaction. However, it is proper to define the extent of services in light of the client's ability to pay. A lawyer should not exploit a fee arrangement based primarily on hourly charges by using wasteful procedures. When there is doubt whether a contingent fee is consistent with the client's best interest, the lawyer should offer the client alternative bases for the fee and explain their implications. Applicable law may impose limitations on contingent fees, such as a ceiling on the percentage.

### Division of Fee

A division of fee is a single billing to a client covering the fee of two or more lawyers who are not in the same firm. A division of fee facilitates association of more than one lawyer in a matter in which neither alone could serve the client as well, and most often is used when the fee is contingent and the division is between a referring lawyer and a trial specialist. Paragraph (e) permits the lawyers to divide a fee on either the basis of the proportion of services they render or by agreement between the participating lawyers if all assume responsibility for the representation as a whole and the client is advised and does not object. It does not require disclosure to the client of the share that each lawyer is to receive. Joint responsibility for the representation entitles the obligations stated in Rule 5.1 for purposes of the matter involved.

### Disputes over Fees

If a procedure has been established for resolution of fee disputes, such as an arbitration or mediation procedure established by the bar, the lawyers should conscientiously consider submitting to it. Law may prescribe a procedure for determining a lawyer's fee, for example, in representation of an executor or administrator, a class or a person entitled to a reasonable fee as part of the measure of damages. The lawyer entitled to such a fee and a lawyer representing another party concerned with the fee should comply with the prescribed procedure.

## APPENDIX B

# Resources for Choosing Time and Billing Software

*ABA Journal,* 750 N. Lake Shore Drive, Chicago IL 60611; 312/988-5522. Monthly, with annual special technology review issue. Free to members; $66 for nonmembers.

*ABA Legal Technology Resource Center,* 750 N. Lake Shore Drive, Chicago IL 60611; 312/988-5465. For $10 for ABA members or $30 for nonmembers, the LTRC will send you a packet of information and articles on time and billing software.

*Beyond the Billable Hour: An Anthology of Alternative Billing Methods,* edited by Richard C. Reed. ABA Section of Law Practice Management, 750 N. Lake Shore Drive, Chicago, IL 60611; 312/988-5522; fax: 312/988-5568; $69.95 (LPM Section members), $79.95 (nonmembers).

*Computer Counsel,* 641 Lake Street, Suite 403, Chicago IL 60661; 312/207-6900. A quarterly newsletter on law office automation.

*Network 2d,* ABA Section of Law Practice Management, 750 N. Lake Shore Drive, Chicago IL 60611; 312/988-5619. A quarterly newsletter on law-office automation from the Computer and Technology Division.

*Law Office Computing,* James Publishing, Inc., P. O. Box 25202, Santa Ana CA 92799; 714/755-5450. A bimonthly magazine about law-office-based computing systems. $54 yearly.

*The Lawyers PC,* Shepard's/McGraw-Hill, Inc., P.O. Box 35300, Colorado Springs CO 80935-3530; 1-800/525-2474. A bimonthly magazine with hands-on discussions of software and hardware. $105 yearly plus $12 shipping.

**Mentors Directory,** ABA Section of Law Practice Management Solo and Small Firm Coordinating Committee, 750 N. Lake Shore Drive, Chicago IL 60611; 312/988-5646. The Mentors Directory includes names of lawyers and consultants who provide information at no charge. Some are full-time practicing lawyers, others are lawyers who practice law and consult, and others are nonlawyer consultants.

**National Law Journal,** 345 Park Ave. South, New York, NY 10010; 800/888-8300. Special issues devoted to software and legal technology three times a year. Weekly, $124 a year.

**Win-Win Billing Strategies: Alternatives That Satisfy Your Clients and You,** edited by Richard C. Reed. ABA Section of Law Practice Management, 750 N. Lake Shore Drive, Chicago, IL 60611; 312/988-5522; fax: 312/988-5568; $89.95 (LPM Section members), $99.95 (nonmembers).

**WORD Progress,** ABA Section of Law Practice Management, 750 N. Lake Shore Drive, Chicago IL 60611; 312/988-5619. A quarterly newsletter on law-office automation from the Computer and Technology Division.

# Index

## A

Abbreviations, avoiding, 46
Ability to pay, importance of, to clients, 2
Administration, 20
Advance payment, 56–57
    accounting for, with the client, 6
    startup funds, 6
Agreement with the client, 4, 6–15
American Bar Association, on professional conduct, Rule 1.5, 55–57
Assessment, initial, 3

## B

Blocking, to project effort, 27, 46
    example, 28
Budgeting, 20–21

## C

Case, difficulty of, importance to clients, 2. *See also* Story
Client
    concerns of, 2, 4, 47–48
    copying information to, 39–40
    as an individual, concern of lawyer about, 23
Comfort factor, 4
Comment form, 65
Communication, 2–6
    costs of, 32
    of value, 23–37

    *See also* Interaction
Competence
    concern about
        client's, 2, 4
        lawyer's, 3
    demonstrating in bill detail, 30, 45
        example, 31
Completeness, of description on bills, 35–36
Component billing, 17, 32–33
Computer software
    billing for use of, 19–20, 33
    resources for choosing, 59–60
Computer systems, billing for use of, 33
Conference, via telephone, 46
Contingent fee, 55
    appropriate circumstances for using, 56
Contract, covering legal services, 4
Corporate clients, 5
    personalized billing to, 34, 47
Credibility, tracking systems for maintaining, 14

## D

Date of work done, 34, 46
Delegation, estimating cost of, 20
Depositions, benefits of copying to clients, 39–40
Dictation, of time information, 50
Disputes over fees, 57
Division of fees, 56, 57
Document construction, alternative ways to account for, 32

**E**

Editing bills, minimizing, 50
Effectiveness, in billing, 50
Efficiency, concern about
   client's, 2–3
   lawyer's, 3
Effort
   as concern with client's needs, 3
   delineating work done, 23–26
      example, 24–25
   determining, 5
   importance to clients, 2
   projecting in bills, 1, 23–30, 45, 52
      example, 7–13, 33–34
      techniques for, 39–43
      visual strategy for, 27–30
Estimate
   notifying client of changes, 53
   strategy for presenting, 4, 31–32
   written, 14, 55
Ethics
   concern about, client's, 2, 4
   demonstrating integrity, 3
   projecting in billing, 30, 45
Expenses
   listing for clients, example, 9–10,
      12–13
   reimbursable, basis of, 35

**F**

Fee
   American Bar Association model rule,
     55–57
   basis of, communicating to the
     client, 56
   disputes over, 57
   division of, 57
   fairness of

     client's perception, 45
     lawyer's concern about, 3
     projecting, 31–32
   mandatory schedules, 17
   timing of discussions about, 3–4
   voluntary schedules, internal, 17
Fee agreement, 6–14
   example, 15
Fee-schedule mentality, 17
Format, for billing, 32–33
Forms
   computer-generated, charge for
     creating, 19
   fee agreement, 15

**G**

Goals, in preparing bills, 45

**H**

Habit, in timekeeping, 42–43
Honesty. *See* Ethics

**I**

Interaction
   discussing the fee, 4–6
   first meeting, 3
   lawyer's concern in, 3
     demonstrating in billing, 45
     about the individual, 23
   personal, and fee discussion, 5
   personalizing bills, 34
   referencing discussions to convey
     concern, example, 26
   undivided attention to the client, 40
   updating estimates, 6, 31–32
     before mailing bills, 51

**L**

Lawyering, 20
Lawyers
    income of, 20
    rules for division of fees, 56, 57
    *See also* Interaction
"Legal Needs of the Public, The"
    (Curran), 45
Lexis, 19

**M**

Machines, billing for services of, 18–20
Management, literature references and
    order form, 62–63
Missouri Motivational Study, Prentice-
    Hall, 1–2, 45
    on clients willingness to return to
        same lawyer, 47–48
    reasons for using lawyers' services, 3–4
    on timing of fee discussions, 4–5
Morgan, J. Harris, 53
Motivation, of the client in retaining
    services, 1–2

**O**

Overhead, establishing rates for, 18–20

**P**

Payment, terms of, 56–57. *See also*
    Advance
        payment
PCTime (computer software), 50
Personalization of bills, 34, 47
    examples, 35–37
Photocopies, 18
Postage, metering, 18

Preparation of bills, 17–21
Printers, billing for use of, 18–19
Punctuation, to project effort, 27, 46
    example, 28

**R**

Reasonableness of a fee, factors
    determining, 55
Records, content of, 40
References, literature, list of, 62–63
Referral, and integrity, 3
Relationship, client-lawyer, 1–16. *See also*
    Client; Interaction; Lawyers
Research, computerized, charge for, 19,
    32–33
Responsibility, billing for acceptance of,
    47
Results, importance to clients, 2

**S**

Semantics, of projecting effort, 27. *See
    also* Punctuation; Verbs to convey
    action; Word usage
Service rendered
    components of, 20
    as a measure of effort, 5–6, 43
    value of, factors in, 47
    *See also* Effort
Shellenberger, Fran, 53
Size, physical, of bill, 27–30, 46–47
Software
    billing for use of, 33
    resources for choosing, 59–60
    for timekeeping, 49–50
Specificity, in billing, 23
Staff, billing for services of, 18
Story of the case, 2

plot, construction of, 40
    telling in a paragraph billing, 43
Supreme Court, on mandatory fee
    schedules, 17

## T

Tamminen, Julie M., 53
Telephone calls
    conference, 46
    cost of managing, 18, 32
Texas Bar, study of fees, 5
Time
    as a measure of effort, 5
    recording on bills, 47
    statement of, example, 7–10
Time and motion studies, 17
Timekeeping, 49–51
    system for, 40–43
        software, 49
Timeliness, in maintaining records,
    49–51
Timeslips (computer software), 49
Timing, for presenting a final bill, 14,
    34–35
Tracking systems, establishing

credibility by explaining, 14
Trust account for fees, 6
    accounting for, 30

## V

Value
    communicating, 23–37
    meanings of, 17
    of service rendered, 47
Values, projecting in billing, example,
    31
Verbs to convey action, 27, 45–46, 50
    example, 29–30
    *See also* Word usage

## W

Westlaw, 19
Word processing, 20
Word usage, 45–47
    briefed versus researched, 31
    competence communicated through
        terminology, 3
    in formatting the bill, 32
    *See also* Verbs to convey action

# Selected Books From...

**ABA Guide to International Business Negotiations.** A guide to the general, legal, and cultural issues that arise during international negotiations.

**ABA Guide to Legal Marketing.** A collection of new and innovative marketing ideas and strategies for lawyers and firms.

**Becoming Computer Literate.** A guide to computer basics for lawyers and other legal professionals.

**Breaking Traditions.** A guide to progressive, flexible, and sensible work alternatives for lawyers who want to balance the demand of the legal profession with other commitments. Model policy for childbirth and parenting leave is included.

**Changing Jobs, 2nd Ed.** A handbook designed to help lawyers make changes in their professional careers. Includes career planning advice from nearly 50 experts.

**Compensation Plans for Law Firms, 2nd Ed.** This second edition discusses the basics for a fair and simple compensation system for partners, of counsel, associates, paralegals, and staff.

**Do-It-Yourself Public Relations.** A hands-on guide for lawyers with public relations ideas, sample letters and forms. The book includes a diskette that includes model letters to the press that have paid off in news stories and media attention.

**Finding the Right Lawyer.** A guide that answers the questions people need to ask when searching for legal counsel. It includes a glossary of legal specialties and the ten questions you should ask a lawyer before hiring.

**Flying Solo: A Survival Guide for the Solo Lawyer, 2nd Ed.** An updated and expanded guide to the problems and issues unique to the solo practitioner.

**How to Draft Bills Clients Rush to Pay.** A collection of techniques for drafting bills that project honesty, competence, fairness and value and how draft an inviting statement.

**How to Start and Build a Law Practice, 3rd Ed.** Jay Foonberg's classic guide has been updated and expanded. Included are more than 10 new chapters on marketing, financing, automation, practicing from home, ethics and professional responsibility.

**Introduction to Desktop Publishing.** .A concise guide to learning the essential elements, techniques, and advantages of desktop publishing.

**Law Office Staff Manual for Solos and Small Law Firms.** A book to help solo and small firm practitioners set up their own law office staff manuals. It includes a diskette containing the text of the manual. The diskette is in WordPerfect 5.1 and ASCII formats.

**Lawyer's Guide to the Internet.** A no-nonsense guide to what the Internet is (and isn't), how it applies to the legal profession, and the different ways it can -- and should -- be used.

**Leveraging with Legal Assistants.** Reviews the changes that have led to increased use of legal assistants and the need to enlarge their role further. Learn specific ways in which a legal assistant can handle a substantial portion of traditional lawyer work.

**LOCATE, 1995-96.** Co-published with the Association of Legal Administrators. It includes about 140 vendors, 300-400 different software products, and totally revamped listings that will make it easy for you to find the right software.

**Microsoft® Word for Windows® in One Hour for Lawyers.** This book includes special tips for users of Windows 95. It contains four easy lessons--timed at 15 minutes each--that will help lawyers prepare, save, and edit a basic document.

**Results-Oriented Financial Management.** A Guide to Successful Law Firm Financial Performance. How to manage "the numbers," from setting rates and computing billable hours to calculating net income and preparing the budget. Over 30 charts and statements to help you prepare reports.

**Through the Client's Eyes: New Approaches to Get Clients to Hire You Again and Again.** Includes an overview of client relations and sample letters, surveys, and self-assessment questions to gauge your client relations acumen.

**TQM in Action: One Firm's Journey Toward Quality and Excellence.** A guide to implementing the principles of Total Quality Management in your law firm.

**Win-Win Billing Strategies.** Represents the first comprehensive analysis of what constitutes "value," and how to bill for it. You'll learn how to initiate and implement different billing methods that make sense for you and your client.

**Winning with Computers, Part 1.** Addresses virtually every aspect of the use of computers in litigation. You'll get an overview of products available and tips on how to put them to good use. For the beginning and advanced computer user.

**Winning with Computers, Part 2.** Expands on the ways you can use computers to manage the routine and not-so-routine aspects of your trial practice. Learn how to apply general purpose software and even how to have fun with your computer.

**Women Rainmakers' 101+ Best Marketing Tips.** A collection of over 130 marketing tips suggested by women rainmakers throughout the country. Includes tips on image, networking, public relations, and advertising.

**WordPerfect® 6.1 for Windows® in One Hour for Lawyers.** This is a crash course in the most popular word processing software package used by lawyers. In four lessons, you'll learn the basic steps for getting a simple job done.

**WordPerfect® Shortcuts for Lawyers: Learning Merge and Macros in One Hour.** A fast-track guide to two of WordPerfect's more advanced functions: merge and macros. Includes 4 lessons designed to take 15 minutes each.

# Order Form

| Qty | Title | LPM Price | Regular Price | Total |
|-----|-------|-----------|---------------|-------|
| _____ | ABA Guide to Int'l Business Negotiations (511-0331) | $ 74.95 | $ 84.95 | $_____ |
| _____ | ABA Guide to Legal Marketing (511-0341) | 69.95 | 79.95 | $_____ |
| _____ | Becoming Computer Literate (511-0342) | 32.95 | 39.95 | $_____ |
| _____ | Breaking Traditions (511-0320) | 64.95 | 74.95 | $_____ |
| _____ | Changing Jobs, 2nd Ed. (511-0334) | 49.95 | 59.95 | $_____ |
| _____ | Compensation Plans for Lawyers (511-0353) | 69.95 | 79.95 | $_____ |
| _____ | Do-It-Yourself Public Relations (511-0352) | 69.95 | 79.95 | $_____ |
| _____ | Finding the Right Lawyer (511-0339) | 19.95 | 19.95 | $_____ |
| _____ | Flying Solo, 2nd Ed. (511-0328) | 59.95 | 69.95 | $_____ |
| _____ | How to Draft Bills Clients Rush to Pay (511-0344) | 39.95 | 49.95 | $_____ |
| _____ | How to Start & Build a Law Practice, 3rd Ed. (511-0293) | 32.95 | 39.95 | $_____ |
| _____ | Introduction to Desktop Publishing (511-0357) | 19.95 | 29.95 | $_____ |
| _____ | Law Office Staff Manual for Solos & Small Firms (511-0361) | 49.95 | 59.95 | $_____ |
| _____ | Lawyer's Guide to the Internet (511-0343) | 24.95 | 29.95 | $_____ |
| _____ | Leveraging with Legal Assistants (511-0322) | 59.95 | 69.95 | $_____ |
| _____ | LOCATE 1995-96 (511-0359) | 65.00 | 75.00 | $_____ |
| _____ | Microsoft® Word for Windows® in One Hour (511-0358) | 19.95 | 29.95 | $_____ |
| _____ | Results-Oriented Financial Management (511-0319) | 44.95 | 54.95 | $_____ |
| _____ | Through the Client's Eyes (511-0337) | 69.95 | 79.95 | $_____ |
| _____ | TQM in Action (511-0323) | 59.95 | 69.95 | $_____ |
| _____ | Win-Win Billing Strategies (511-0304) | 89.95 | 99.95 | $_____ |
| _____ | Winning with Computers, Part 1 (511-0294) | 89.95 | 99.95 | $_____ |
| _____ | Winning with Computers, Part 2 (511-0315) | 59.95 | 69.95 | $_____ |
| _____ | Winning with Computers, Parts 1 & 2 (511-0316) | 124.90 | 144.90 | $_____ |
| _____ | Women Rainmakers' 101+ Best Marketing Tips (511-0336) | 14.95 | 19.95 | $_____ |
| _____ | WordPerfect® 6.1 for Windows® in One Hour for Lawyers (511-0354) | 19.95 | 29.95 | $_____ |
| _____ | WordPerfect® Shortcuts for Lawyers (511-0329) | 14.95 | 19.95 | $_____ |

**\*HANDLING**

| | |
|--|--|
| $ 2.00-$9.99 | $2.00 |
| 10.00-24.99 | $3.95 |
| 25.00-49.99 | $4.95 |
| 50.00 + | $5.95 |

**\*\*TAX**

DC residents add 5.75%
IL residents add 8.75%
MD residents add 5%

SUBTOTAL: $_____
\*HANDLING: $_____
\*\*TAX: $_____

TOTAL: $_____

## PAYMENT

☐ Check enclosed (Payable to the ABA)     ☐ Bill Me

☐ Visa     ☐ MasterCard Account Number:_____-_____-_____-_____

☐ American Express     Exp. Date: _____ Signature _____

Name_____

Firm_____

Address_____

City_____State_____ZIP_____

Phone number_____

**Mail to:** ABA, Publication Orders, P.O. Box 10892, Chicago, IL 60610-0892

**Phone:** (312) 988-5522     **Fax:** (312) 988-5568
Email:abasvcctr@attmail.com     World WideWeb: http//www.abanet.org/lpm/catalog     BOOK

# CUSTOMER COMMENT FORM

Title of Book:_____

We've tried to make this publication as useful, accurate, and readable as possible. Please take 5 munutes to tell us if we succeeded. Your comments and suggestions will help us improve our publications. Thank you!

1. How did you acquire this publication:

☐ by mail order     ☐ at a meeting/convention     ☐ as a gift

☐ by phone order     ☐ at a bookstore     ☐ don't know

☐ other: (describe)_____
_____

Please rate this publication as follows:

| | Excellent | Good | Fair | Poor | Not Applicable |
|---|---|---|---|---|---|
| **Readability:** Was the book easy to read and understand? | ☐ | ☐ | ☐ | ☐ | ☐ |
| **Examples/Cases:** Were they helpful, practical? Were there enough? | ☐ | ☐ | ☐ | ☐ | ☐ |
| **Content:** Did the book meet your expectations? Did it cover the subject adequately? | ☐ | ☐ | ☐ | ☐ | ☐ |
| **Organization and clarity:** Was the sequence of text logical? Was it easy to find what you wanted to know? | ☐ | ☐ | ☐ | ☐ | ☐ |
| **Illustrations/forms/checklists:** Were they clear and useful? Were there enough? | ☐ | ☐ | ☐ | ☐ | ☐ |
| **Physical attractiveness:** What did you think of the appearance of the publication (typesetting, printing, etc.)? | ☐ | ☐ | ☐ | ☐ | ☐ |

Would you recommend this book to another attorney/administrator? ☐ Yes ☐ No

How could this publication be improved? What else would you like to see in it?

_____
_____
_____

Do you have other comments or suggestions?_____
_____
_____

Name_____

Firm/Company_____

Address_____

City/State/ZIP_____ Phone_____

Firm Size_____ Area of specialization_____

**We appreciate your time and help.**

**Fold**

**BUSINESS REPLY MAIL**

FIRST CLASS      PERMIT NO. 16471      CHICAGO, ILLINOIS

*POSTAGE WILL BE PAID BY ADDRESSEE*

AMERICAN BAR ASSOCIATION
PPM, 8TH FLOOR
750 N. LAKE SHORE DRIVE
CHICAGO, ILLINOIS 60611-9851

NO POSTAGE
NECESSARY
IF MAILED
IN THE
UNITED STATES

**Fold**